My Birth Dad
was a
Righteous Brother

My Adoption Journey

A Story by

Sheri L. Strobaugh

Table of Contents

Dedication

I dedicate this book to my beautiful family. My loving husband of over forty years, Pete. You have always believed in me and as a writer. To my three beautiful children, Brandon, Sarah and Nick. You have supported me 100% through this journey. And to my five grandchildren, Evan, Olivia, Nathan, Annie and Jordynn. Thank you for loving your Mimi!

I also dedicate this book to Bobby Hatfield, my birth Father. I had no idea what a thrill it would be to look like someone so much and to have the same certain characteristics. It still blows me away. I hope you are looking down from Heaven with love, knowing that I turned out fine and have been blessed with such a beautiful family. Thank you for having me.

Preface

This is a story about my adoption journey. It is not a tell all book nor do I have any intention of hurting any feelings. This is about me and what I have gone through as I discovered my birth family. All of the incredible emotions I went through and did not understand. All of the insecurities that creeped out of me when I least expected it. All of the bouts of unbelievable joy and sorrow. Knowing that there are so many like me out there, not knowing if they have the stomach or nerve to search.

I have decided to delete everything pertaining to my birth mother to protect her privacy as she is still living.

Part One

Non-Identification

Chapter **1**

Man, do I have a story!!! Never in my wildest dreams could I have guessed that wanting to know my background would lead to writing a book! But honestly, I feel I must share my story because I know there are hundreds of thousands of adoptees who have gone or are going through what I am going through.

I know it's hard to believe that others feel the way I do but I'm sure they do or you do. I have read so many adoption stories over the years and cried tears of joy but also tears for some of the sad, sad endings. Also, it's almost impossible to have patience when you decide to search, but you have no choice. Time can feel like it is totally standing still!

Let me tell you my story…

My brother-in-law died of a heart attack in June 2006. He was only 62 years old, not overweight, didn't drink or smoke, but perhaps indulged in the good foods of life. I don't know.

Who would have guessed that we would lose him just like that? I loved him dearly and knew him for 30 years. He was 12 years older than my husband. They were so close. His life was gone in an instant.

They were supposed to come up in August and stay with us like they do every year. What a tragedy. Heaven is very lucky to have him! We use to sit around the living room and just laugh over old stories of us growing up and stupid things that we did. We had a very special yearly visit.

They were planning on moving up here and we spent many times driving around the area trying to find a place for them to relocate. They just weren't totally ready to commit. The weather was one factor. Moving from Sacramento to Seattle was a BIG change, no doubt. So, losing John was a shocking, devastating and mostly sad, sad thing for us. Who would have thought that would happen to us, to his wife and to his children?

I remember the day I got the call. I was at work. Pete (my hubby) told me that his brother, J.B., had died of a heart attack. Ugh, what a sick feeling. I couldn't stop the tears. I told him that we would fly down with him to be with his wife and family. My boss didn't hesitate to give me the time off.

We made it through and spent many hours reminiscing, crying and laughing. It was hard to leave my sister-in-law, Karen, but she had her children who would keep an eye on her. John Benton Strobaugh, you are truly going to be missed.

Because of his death, I knew that I needed to find out about any health issues my birth family may have had. My Dad thought it was a good idea. He also said that since I worked at an Indian Casino, it would be smart to find out how much native blood I have. It would give me more job protection, but that is a completely different story! So, my Dad called the adoption agency for me. He gave me the number of the lady who handles the non-ids (Non-Identifying Background Information).

My Mom said, "It makes me uncomfortable that you're getting your non-id." I told her not to worry and that I needed to find out medical issues. Why wouldn't she want me to know if there was cancer or any other worries in the family. She just really didn't want me to have any contact with Children's Home Society, the adoption agency at all.

My mother has never offered any information about my adoption except she told me that my parents were 17 years old and I have English and Dutch blood with perhaps a bit of Indian. I was the one who always brought it up. Not too frequently, just here and there over the years. She also told me that my birth Father had brothers who were football players and well over six foot tall. It was very possible that I could have tall children.

I'm only 5"4."

Chapter 2

I called the adoption agency and the gal was really nice and said she would send the information I needed to fill out to get started on obtaining my non-id. It took a very long week to get it. I don't know why I was so anxious.

When I went to the local notary with my paperwork, I had a knot in my stomach. I was asking for information on my birth family! I had my signature notarized and kept waiting for a look from the notary, just a hint that I was trying to find out something exciting. Did she have any idea that this was a HUGE thing for me? I don't think so. She was verifying who I was by my license. I walked out the door with a notarized document showing that I want my non-identifying information on my birth family.

Very unexpectedly, a bolt of lightning shot through my body! If I could have skipped down the street without looking like a complete lunatic, I would have. Why was I so excited? It's just a non-id. I sent off my notarized paperwork and the $100.00

fee to receive my information. I was nervous and excited at the same time.

On July 27, 2006, I received a letter from Children's Home Society of California. The Society thanked me for my recent correspondence and noted receipt of my waiver of rights to confidentiality for siblings and Notarized Consent for Contact. The letter further stated that CHS has not received a matching Consent from either my birth parents, or a matching sibling waiver.

For some reason tears came to my eyes. I felt extremely depressed at the reality that once I was given up, I was not sought after. And believe me, I have wonderful parents and have had a great childhood. I have no idea why this hit me so deeply. I found myself in tears a few more times throughout the day, not to the knowledge of my husband or kids. I felt silly sharing an emotion I didn't even understand myself.

The letter further stated that they had received my $100.00 and request for my non-id record review and written report. They would complete it as quickly as possible for me, but they anticipated that my request would require approximately six months to process. I figured it was time for me to have some patience and get on with business as usual. Maybe by the New Year, I'd receive my highly anticipated non-identification report. That would be a great New Year's gift!

Chapter 3

About 8 weeks later, I needed to pick up my husband who was just flying back from Alaska. He had been working up there for a few months. It was an exciting day! He flew my youngest son, Nicky, and I up about six weeks ago for a week. He had rented a cabin on an island and we could only get there by boat. That was very cool. We had some great campfires, went fishing a couple of times, saw a few bears and had some great meals. What a terrific time. Now it was time for him to come home to his family. He had finished his job.

I had forgotten to check the mail today so on the way out to the airport, I grabbed it. I glanced through my mail, looking for something besides the usual bills and junk mail and there IT was…a package from The Children's Home Society of California! Oh, my gosh! It's here already? Four months early? My heart leapt to my throat; my pulse was racing while my stomach churned at the same time. Would I open it, could I open it? I wasn't supposed to get it until New Years!

I laid it on the passenger seat and proceeded to drive to SeaTac airport just south of Seattle. I kept looking and touching the package as I drove. I must have glanced at the envelope 500 times in the hour and twenty minutes it took me to get there. Traffic was amazingly smooth, so I arrived about 40 minutes early. I found a parking spot in the parking garage.

Well, there it was, just me and the taunting envelope, waiting to be opened...

So many things went through my mind. Will it be the same story my parents have told throughout my life? Were they high school sweethearts and only 17? Was my birth Dad athletic and did he have a brother 6'2" who played football? Am I Dutch and English? Will there just be statistics about illnesses in the family and nothing personal? Only one way to find out, I guess.

Okay, it was time to get it together. All I had to do was open the envelope. I picked it up and stared blankly for a few more minutes. I slowly opened it. I took a deep breath.

It was several pages long, more than I had expected. It started out about my birth mother who was 17 years old. All right, I knew that. It's all good. Then it said she was of Dutch and Irish decent with a small amount of American Indian. "Wait a sec, Irish? Irish? I'm Irish?" That's very cool. How fun is that?

My birth Mom was 5'3" with blue eyes and brown hair and weighed 112 lbs. I couldn't read anymore because my eyes had filled up with tears. Why was this making me emotional? Was I just tired?

Dabbing my eyes, trying not to smear my mascara, (I wanted to look good for my husband), I read further. This is where I have decided to delete. There were so many coincidences between her and I regarding school activities. I hope you understand. I'm so glad I was alone. This was too personal to share right away. If I couldn't understand my feelings, how could I explain them?

My maternal grandfather was of Irish descent, about 6 feet tall and had black hair with blue eyes...my oldest son has black hair and blue eyes. I have always wondered about Brandon's looks. Although he looks so much like my husband, the black hair with the blue eyes is very striking.

My maternal grandmother was of Dutch descent with dark brown hair and green eyes. Both grandparents were in good health. That was good news to hear my birth grandparents were in good health. That is part of the reason I ordered this non-identification.

There was no diabetes, allergies or mental illness in my maternal health history. That is good to know. I had to read about my maternal family about 3 times before I could venture on to my birth Father and his family. These aren't just statistics! These people became real and made me wonder if I looked like any of them. Do I have someone's smile? Or maybe their sassy sense of humor or even the same nose? Are they just waiting for me to contact them? Do they think of me on my birthday?

My birth Father was 17 years of age and was born in either Colorado or Utah and was of Swedish descent. Wait a minute…now I'm Swedish too?? Holy cow! People have always asked me if I was Swedish. I always just said, "Nope, Dutch, English, Indian".

Back to my birth Dad. He was approximately 5'9", medium build with thin blonde hair and blue eyes. He had a fair complexion. The records indicated that he was good in sports and also very artistic. His health was good.

You may find this funny, but I am picturing Hutch from Starsky and Hutch. His name is David Soul although I think he's a lot bigger and I'm not sure what color of eyes he has. I'm pretty athletic and fairly artistic. Hmmm… This is definitely not what I expected. Where is my Dad now? What if I decide to contact him? It would devastate my Mom. I have to not think about that right now. I can't think logically while I'm on overload! Okay Sheri, just read some more.

My paternal grandfather was of Swedish descent and was 6'4", medium build with blue eyes and a medium complexion. He owned a "cleaners" business. He was in good health. My paternal grandmother was 5'3" with thin dark blonde hair and blue eyes with a very fair complexion and of Swedish descent. He had two brothers at the time of my birth. One was 23, 6'5" with dark blonde hair and blue eyes. The other brother was 16, 5'10" with blonde hair and blue eyes. They were all in good health with no diabetes, allergies or mental illness. Yahoo, no mental illness! I am feeling relieved that there isn't too much to report. I just wonder how thoroughly the adoption agency interviewed the families or did all the information come from what my birth Mom knew?

And there I had it. A family I have never known and would never meet. Do they think about me? Do they know my birthday is May 1st?? Do they want to pretend I never happened? Do they ever pray for me? Once again it was time for more tissue. Am I over feeling this? Did anyone else go through my same feelings? Why should I care so much? I don't know these people. I don't even know their names. Read on Sheri.

The report stated that my birth parents were single, and they had no children prior to me. They dated over a period of time and had a meaningful relationship. It further stated that my birth Father was aware of the pregnancy and they both felt they were too young for the responsibilities of a marriage and family.

In order to keep the pregnancy concealed from her friends and community, my birth mother relocated to a new area. Although a difficult decision, my birth mother and her mother contacted The Children's Home Society approximately 5 months prior to my birth. So that was that.

Now I'm thinking...In order to conceal from friends and family...wow I know things were different back then, but keep it from family? I would think my birth Mom could use all the support she could get. And I wonder what they told anyone, maybe just the family? Can you really keep a secret like that? I am just grateful that she chose to have me. She has given me life and I will always remember that and be thankful. I have had a wonderful life with a beautiful family, kids and grandkids.

I was born May 1, 1958 at 9:18 pm at a hospital in Los Angeles. I was 6 pounds, 10 ounces and 19 inches long. My birth Mom was in labor 6 hours. The records indicate that I was in excellent physical development. I had dark curly hair; large, dark blue eyes; and a little, turned up nose. I was described as a very attractive baby girl, who did a considerable amount of looking about for a baby my age. Well, aren't I something!

My birth mother signed the relinquishment papers two weeks after my birth. I remained in the care of CHS foster family until I went to live with my adoptive family on June 10, 1958. So, for six weeks I was with a foster family. Those are amazing people. I would be so attached after six weeks. It takes some special people to do foster care I'm sure. I wish I could thank my foster caregivers personally.

My brother David was excited to meet me. He wanted to take me home right away. That is good to know. Some two-year-old's would be very jealous. My Mom lucked out. Evidently, I thoroughly eye-balled my Mom, Dad and Brother for an extended period of time…which made me quite advanced for my age. That cracked me up that they wrote that.

My adoption was granted on March 3, 1959. Wow, my Mom had to wait nine months before legally adopting me. That had to be hard knowing that I could get taken away prior to that. Such a process! I know it was such an emotional time for my Mom. She said she knew I was hers but couldn't feel completely happy until they signed the papers. She said she was so relieved to know that the birth mother hadn't changed her mind. I can imagine the knot she had in her stomach for so long. She knew she loved me and that I was a gift from God but had to wait because of all the legalities.

Again, it stated that there was no documentation of contact with either of my birth parents since the time of my adoption. Okay, don't rub it in.

What a way to end it. Now I'm feeling depressed again. Thanks for reminding me that they chose never to contact me again. Get over it Sheri. I read it all again and let this information sink in. I read it once more and then it was time to meet my husband.

When I got to the baggage pick up where I was to meet him, I saw that his flight had been delayed another 30 minutes. Back to my letter. I found a spot away from others and read my non-id again. Who would have thought that so much information would have been passed to me?

As I looked around at the hustle and bustle of the airport, no one has any idea what I am going through. Friends and family are meeting with smiles and hugs and some with weary eyes. The thought just occurred to me; will this ever be me meeting my birth family for the first time? Okay I am getting ahead of myself. I don't know if I will ever make contact. Who knows if I could even find them if I tried? My mind is all over the place. It was cool to watch all of the reunions at the airport though.

The reunion with my husband was wonderful! He was a beautiful sight for sore eyes. He was home. Halleluiah!! He wasn't going to do that again. It was too hard to be away. The money was great, but who cares.

When we got to the car I told him about the letter. I drove so he could read it. He was dumbfounded and didn't know what to say. I said that I thought it would be a good idea to read this letter to the kids and let them know they were Swedish and Irish too. But first they had to celebrate their Dad's homecoming.

Chapter 4

The next night, we had a family dinner. My kids knew I sent off for the non-id but they thought I would just be getting medical facts etc. We were sitting around the dinner table and I asked my daughter to read the letter aloud. She read all three pages and as I looked around, everyone had a smile on their face. When she got to the part of the maternal grandfather having black hair and blue eyes, I looked at Brandon (my oldest) and said, "So that's where you get those looks, crazy huh?"

It was a great evening. The kids were trying to grasp the fact that they were Swedish and Irish too. I don't really know what they were thinking. They've always known I was adopted, and the Grandparents were always the Grandparents. I was feeling pretty dang good about sharing everything with the family. I felt so connected with each word on the non-id papers. This was my history, my legacy. These were my blood relatives. I felt warmth and shivers at the same time.

Towards the end of the evening, I pulled my daughter Sarah into my bedroom. I told her that I had way too much curiosity going on and I will probably try to search for my birth parents. I told her that this was so very personal, and I don't know if I could let it go. We were alone and she could see the excitement in my eyes. She said to go for it and see what happens. I explained that it would be a long process and perhaps I would never find out. I just needed to talk to someone about it. I had told my husband but needed to talk more! My daughter will support whatever I do just as well as my two boys. I can't describe the feeling of my decision. Ecstatic doesn't even start to describe it.

So, it's now a few days after our wonderful dinner and I'm at work. I decide to take a break and get on the computer. I spent the last few hours working on schedules. I needed a break.

Chapter 5

I got on the computer and googled "How to I find my birth family?" Google came up with several sights, but one was California Search Angels. That clicked with me. I found a certain search angel for California and sent off an email. I heard back from Bob, Donna and Connie, my search angels right away! Even before my break was over. Super cool! I explained my situation. They wanted to know my non-id information. I gave them all the information that I had. I had heard about people searching and understand that it takes about a year to get the information...if at all.

I was so excited that they got back to me the same day. I thought I would have time to prepare. Okay, I am getting ahead of myself again. I gave them my information including my mother's maiden name. They asked me where I was born, and I told them Los Angeles.

I heard back that Los Angeles was a pain to figure out because I might be listed twice but Bob thought that Donna might be able to help. I then gave Donna all of the information that I had.

Donna said there were several listings for other females born in Los Angeles on that day so I wasn't alone. They came up with 5 names and possibilities and none of them clicked with me.

The names, Lessor, Jones, Cordes, Blackburn and Bundy (Yikes!) just didn't strike that note. I wasn't feeling anything. That doesn't mean they weren't my birth family; I just didn't feel anything. I was told the main gal that could help me further was out of state for two weeks, but they had another gal who could do a thorough search for a cost. Was I willing to wait that long? At this point, no! A few minutes ago, I felt like things were going too fast. Now I'm not willing to wait two weeks, lol. My brain was feeling scrambled.

I was given Jan's name and she charged $75.00. I talked with my husband and he said to go for it. It's only $75.00 to know my birth name, my birth parents name, any names of my birth siblings if in fact I had any. At least I might find out. Who would have thought my stomach would go through so much? Why was I feeling physically ill?

Right now, I think that $75.00 is a drop in a bucket. This could be life changing. Is there someone out there who looks like me?

Why can I not wait two weeks after all these years? Why can I not show just a bit of patience? I can't answer these questions except to say, I can't wait. I am like a kid in a candy store! I am not even contemplating contacting these people at this point. I may never do that as long as I live. But just the knowledge of knowing my birth name, my birth parents name is so compelling to me now.

I gave Jan the go ahead. Jan was going to do some researching for me. Okay cool, now I just have to be patient and know if it's meant to be, it's meant to be.

Part Two

Discovery

Chapter 6

By October 5, 2006, Jan had my birth information. I'm sitting in my office working on scheduling and various things. I had just come in from doing triple jackpots. The guy got a jackpot and before I could deliver his money, he hit another one! And then a third! I had to pay him out because I was his good luck charm… after all I am Irish!

I decided I needed a break and to check my email. There was a message from Jan! There goes my heart again! Settle down, I'm sure it's nothing.

was wrong. It wasn't "nothing". She said she had information for me. My heart pounded a little harder. I'm looking around the office where I have spent the last 5 years working on schedules, counseling people and just keeping things in a smooth motion. I am going to find out "stuff" right now! I need my family! Dang it, I can't wait…I have to keep on reading.

Before I show you this, I will need to change my birth mother's name. I have just finished this book and feel that it is best, and you will understand as this story unfolds.

I go ahead and start reading and as I do there is such a loud heartbeat in my ears. Okay, there's my name:

Birth Name: Pamela L. Hatfield

Birth Mother's maiden name: Jones

Birth Father: R. L. Hatfield

Birth Certificate Numbers: Local #16464 – State # 101031

Right now, I am bawling my eyes out. I thought I had a year to get ready for this.

Oh, my gosh…I was born Pamela L. Hatfield. My best friend's name is Pamela! I call her Pammy. I think that's such a coincidence! I never thought in my wildest dreams that I would ever know my birth name. I did think about possibly finding information in my parents' files after they had passed. But never my birth name. Pamela Lee Hatfield. I like it. That is a lovely name. Sheri fits me much better though.

My birth Mom's name was Jones…I had a (friend) in high school named Jones. She was not the nicest person in the world…and not really my friend. I just hoped that she wasn't related because you can pick your friends.

The birth Father's name is: R. L. Hatfield…who is R. L. Hatfield? I am still feeling the heartbeat in my ears, thumping away. Does anyone know how I'm feeling right now? Could anyone possibly know? He was not born in California, so it was going to be a little tougher.

Could I just let it go? I NOW know my birth name. Hatfield. No way! I can't let this story just come to an end. I have to finish seeing what happens! Do I have any brothers or sisters out there? Do they even know about me? Do I look like them? This is crazy! I realize my face was drenched. My sleeve came in handy. My mind is going a million places. Hatfield, it just fits and I don't know why. Why did the other names not feel right?

This is the beginning of MY history. A history I have never known about or ever pursued before. Where is this going to lead? Will I ever see my birth family face to face? Will it be like looking in a mirror? I had no idea what simple names on paper would do to me. I want to cry and laugh. I want to be at home and share this with my family.

Chapter 7

Jan really came through for me. The $75.00 dollars I paid for this information was such a minimal amount to find out how I am...Pamela Lee Hatfield. I forwarded this information to Bob, Donna and Connie. I told them I was in shock and it was only just paper and names. I thanked and thanked them. They truly were angels. I knew that with the information Jan found, they would work miracles.

The next day Donna emailed me back. She said, "Take a deep breath. I have lots of information for you. She gave me all of my birth Mom's information, as well as my aunts and uncles etc. I was in overload.

"One more thing. It looks like we have a contact number." She suggested that I keep it light and see if it's a good time to talk. Then I could just see how it goes from there.

(Although I have deleted the parts that include my birth mother, I am keeping the thoughts I had at the time.) Does she want to remember me? Does she think about me? Everyday?

Once a year on my birthday? Do I look like her? I don't know if I could ever get the courage to ask her about that. I don't even know at this point if I am going to make contact.

I had one of my Supervisors listen while I read the email and she was dumbfounded and had no words of wisdom or explanation. That's okay, I didn't expect it. This is a very unusual situation and I have no idea what to think.

Donna also found two possibilities of my birth Father according to the marriage records. One was Ralph L. Hatfield and the other was Robert L. Hatfield. So, funny thought, I grew up with a German Shepard named Ralph who lived across the street so I kind of hope that maybe Robert pans out. Either one would be great if one was really my birth Father. One married in Los Angeles and the other in Riverside. Could one of these really be my birth Dad? Will he want to meet me after all these years?

This was so much information all at once. I want the world to stop for a little while so I can concentrate only on this. I want to be able to cry for hours if I want to or jump for joy or just stare at the ceiling. Well that would be in a perfect world so I guess I will try to cope with it all and just deep breathe. After all, I'm the one that got me into this.

Chapter 8

Now it's the next day, a Sunday afternoon and my mind is still reeling with all the information given to me the day before. My family was in shock too! These Search Angels are pretty incredible and spend hours of their time for free, just to help people like me. I will be grateful to them forever.

It is finally lunch time and I bring my salad to my office. I have a half hour to relax so I thought I would do a little research and get on the internet. Selfishly liking the name Robert over Ralph, and you know why, I decided to look up past Alumni's of high schools in Orange County.

The first one I picked was Anaheim Union High School. I got to the website and went to search for past alumnus. I typed in R. L. Hatfield. What I saw next was something I would have never expected in my wildest dreams! First of all, to find a match on my first try, but secondly for it to show someone famous! It read... past alumni's R. L. "Bobby" Hatfield of the Righteous Brothers! My stomach literally had butterflies swirling around and I noticed my mouth was hanging wide open. Okay, okay, I was getting ahead of myself. Hatfield is a fairly common name.

My girlfriend walked into the office and I had told her what I found. She said to remember how many people live in southern California. She just couldn't imagine that this could be the same R. L. Hatfield. She said, "Sheri, you do realize how huge California is don't you?" I said, "It's really not that big, now sit down! I need someone with me!" Before I click on this name, I start doubting and thinking about the words of my friend. She was just trying to be logical and didn't want me to jump ahead of the horse.

I clicked on his name and it brought me to Wikipedia. I looked at the picture. There he was. Tears… This beautiful man… Tears… who looked JUST LIKE ME. My throat ached from the pounding and my chest felt so tight. What in the world? My girlfriend got tears in her eyes because she saw the man who looked like me. Bobby Hatfield 1940-2003, he passed away 3 years ago! Oh no! Reading that made my whole body feel weighted down. Even though I wasn't sure that he was my birth Dad… I was sure.

I read the article on him. He moved to Anaheim, California when he was four from Wisconsin, not Colorado or Utah. His parents opened a dry cleaner's business. Oh, my gosh!!! I had to pull out my non-identification. Yep, there it was. The grandparents had a "cleaners" business. He had two brothers; my birth Dad had two brothers. He was around 5'9

31

with blonde hair and blue eyes, just like my birth Dad. He almost went pro baseball but chose to pursue his singing career. My birth Dad was athletic and artistic.

For the next hour or two I was completely dumbfounded. I walked around the casino floor and helped guests all the while thinking about my new discovery. On my last break, I printed out the picture and article about Bobby Hatfield. It was called, "Spectropop Remembers Bobby Hatfield, Blue Eyed Soul Brother". The site is done by Peter Richmond. Bobby Hatfield was a music legend. I got on YouTube and looked up the Righteous Brothers. I listened and watched Unchained Melody. I'm not sure that there has ever been a more beautiful voice born on this earth than my birth Dad's.

I then felt so very sad that he had already passed away. I was too late. He would never see how I turned out. I have to believe that things are meant to be, and I should have some faith. Dang it though, why did I wait so long to search? I knew the reason. It was out of respect for my parents.

I finally got off work and headed home. I have a 45-minute commute, but it seemed like forever. I walked in and showed my husband the picture. He looked at me and said, "Sheri, you've found your birth father!" Then I told him who he was. He could only stare at me, now with his mouth hanging open. We are doing a lot of that lately. When he finally spoke, he said that he was shocked that I found out so quickly and all by myself. That was a crazy and sleepless night.

I had to just sit for a while by myself while the rest of the family was fast asleep. I felt numb but bubbly too. Does that make sense?

The next day I thanked the search angels and told them that they didn't need to search for my birth Dad anymore. He was R. L. "Bobby" Hatfield of the Righteous Brothers. They were shocked and thrilled and wished me the best. They said to email them how everything went. They help thousands but rarely does it turn out that an adoptee has a famous birth parent!

Chapter 9

Here I had all this information and my head was over stuffed. My girlfriend couldn't understand why I wouldn't call my birth mother since I had the number. She offered to call her. I thanked her and said, "No!" I told her that I just couldn't do it. I told her that I would never call, ever. I just didn't have it in me. I was not going to take the rejection or be responsible for making the woman who gave me up feel uncomfortable and anguished. My girlfriend did not understand, but my husband did.

My husband knows that I am a very strong woman, but this was something I could not do. He knew it. He knew that there was no way in this world that I would ever call her. There was no way I would subject myself to rejection. My heart kept palpitating just thinking about the possibility. No, I won't do it.

The next day after I got a decent amount of sleep, my husband said he was going to call her. He would talk with her and explain who he was and ask if she would like to speak with me. I told him to do it at his leisure because it wasn't any easy task. I actually didn't want to know when he planned on caller her because I wouldn't be able to function. Was I doing the right thing? Will she be excited? Or will she just hang up on Pete?

Part Three

The Contact

Chapter **10**

I got a call from Pete while I was at work and he said, "Hey hon, I just got off the phone with your birth Mom and she wants to talk with you! She also verified that Bobby was your Dad." I immediately start tearing up again! He said she was going to leave me a message on my cell phone. I sure hope I have a strong heart!

Two major things happened to me today. Contact with my birth mom and Bobby Hatfield really was my Dad. My birth mom verified it. All those times growing up with a hairbrush in my hand while singing in the mirror…

When I got off work, I very nervously checked my messages. There she was. The mother who gave me up for adoption 48 years ago, my birth mom, had left a message.

I didn't have any animosity for her. I knew that it was the right decision for a young girl. She enabled my parents, who couldn't have children, to adopt a child to care, nurture and love. I had a lovely childhood and I have always known I was adopted. A girlfriend once told me that God only gives us as much as we can handle, whether natural or adopted. It's all part of his plan. I wouldn't have wanted it any other way.

Anyway, back to the message. She said, "Hi Sheri. This is *****, your birth mom. I hope you're doing okay with all this. I would like to talk with you so if you would call me when you get home, that would be great".

I hung up the phone and bawled my eyes out while driving down the freeway. Luckily, it's not during traffic time. It's around 8:30 pm at night. I have 45 minutes to let my mind go a million different ways.

Chapter 11

I got home about 10 pm and Pete had a glass of cabernet waiting for me. He said, "Are you ready to call her?" I nodded and we headed upstairs to make the call. It went amazingly smooth. She asked me if I was okay and I asked her the same. She told me that she thought about me every day and prayed for me every night. She continued to tell me that she has felt guilty for the last 48 years. I, first of all, thanked her for having me. I told her that everything was meant to be. I have lived a charmed life. I have a gorgeous husband that I've been married to for 27 years and have had 4 beautiful children. I said that this was the way it was intended. I told her to please not to have any guilt anymore because everything was okay. My parents are absolutely wonderful! Ask anyone!

She seemed to have felt better and our conversation lightened up. We talked for about 45 minutes and I cannot honestly remember what all was said. I think we were both in shock. We exchanged email addresses and promised to send pictures of our families.

I went to bed with a big smile on my face, and an exhausted body. A lot of tears were shed that night. But good tears, relief tears. I did find out she had never told anyone about me.

So now I am going to leave it at that and delete the rest. I am so thankful that she wanted to talk with me. I felt a big burden lift off my shoulders that I didn't know was there.

Chapter 12

It was time to learn more about my birth Dad, Bobby Hatfield. I have three more brothers and another sister! Holy cow, I have three brothers and a sister! Bobby Jr. and Kalin are from his first marriage with Joy. Vallyn and Dustin are from his second marriage with Linda. Will they accept me and just be happy to have me in their lives? Gosh, wouldn't that be great?

By the end of the week, Pete said he found a phone number for Bobby Hatfield Jr., the oldest of Bobby's kids. He was going to make contact on the weekend. Again, I started feeling nervous. He didn't even have to ask me if he should call. Bobby Hatfield was such a legend. I might not get the best reception. If he weren't famous, I wouldn't be as nervous. They could very easily be leery of me and what I want. I can imagine that they might be on the defensive.

What do I want? More family!

Chapter 13

Pete found Bobby Jr.'s phone number after googling for a while. He said that he would call him. Again, I couldn't be around. I was off work, so I had to go outside. He explained who I was.

Bobby said his Dad was all about Rock and Roll and that I was just another facet. He was very blown away by the phone call and finally after about 10 minutes he said that he needed to go talk with his wife. Pete said just give me your email address so my wife can email you. He did. That was kind of disheartening. I so wanted him to be excited that he had another sister out there!

I emailed Bobby Jr. and explained my story and how my whole search went. I sent him the information that the search angels gave me and sent him some pictures of myself. I realized I just invaded his life and who am I to just bomb my way in? I didn't want to interfere with his private life, I just wanted to know if they would be interested to know that they had a sister. He seemed very kind.

Bobby Jr. emailed me back and said that he would be happy to answer any questions I might have. He was very nice about it. He also said that he forwarded my email to his brother, Kalin. I have no idea what Bobby Jr. was thinking. A couple of days later, his wife Kristen sent some pictures to share of their family. That was very thoughtful. They have a beautiful family.

Their oldest son looked like me when I was little.

The next day I heard from my brother, Kalin. He started, "Wow… What a trip." He was excited and curious and blown away. Now THAT'S what I was hoping for! I knew before I ever heard from him that he and I would be the ones who connected. I have always gotten certain feelings about things and people, and this one was strong. He said he was going to wait for the weekend before he contacted his little brother and sister, but he couldn't contain himself and had to let them know about me! He said that my nose, cheeks and smile were a dead ringer with Vallyn. Smile…

Kalin's Aunt Jeanne called him to wish him a Happy Birthday and he gave her the full update on me. She was married to Bobby's oldest brother Carl who died of Alzheimer's the same year Bobby passed away. She did not know about me but just so happens to be really good friends with my birth Mom's sister! That is too weird! Kalin said Aunt Jeanne would be calling me tomorrow. Yay! A new Aunt.

Chapter 14

There were so many ironic things and eerie comparisons which I needed to share. Over the next week, Kalin and I went back and forth learning about each other.

Here's one of the most eerie comparisons... Bobby and Linda got married the SAME DAY and YEAR that Pete and I walked down the aisle. I didn't realize that until the day Kalin emailed me. I was so concerned with liking the name Robert better than Ralph, I didn't even notice the date. My special anniversary date. While my soon to be, husband and I were getting ready for the biggest day in our lives, so was my birth Dad. That is just too crazy right there. You have to agree. Another thing is they all used to hang out at Corona Del Mar. That was our beach too! Mom used to take us every weekend to Corona.

What an odd feeling that Bobby could have been on the next towel over. Or maybe he loved to bodysurf like I did. I wouldn't get out of the water until my lips turned blue. As soon as they "pinked up", off I went back into the ocean.

I was just in Corona Del Mar, Newport Beach and Laguna two months before I found out who I was. I came down for my 30th High School Reunion. I brought my daughter and best friend to my favorite beach, Corona Del Mar. They loved it too.

Kalin told his Mom about me and asked her if she knew about me. She answered that she DID know about me. Vallyn told her Mom about me and ask her if she knew about me. She DID know about me too. I hope some time I will have the opportunity to have lunch with them. Separately, of course. It would be just nice to know how he told them about me and what his perspective was.

Kalin was curious about my birth mother and asked what she was like and when she knew Dad. I filled him in as much as I knew.

That night I had some weird dreams. They were mainly about how much my birth Dad and I looked alike. I am proud of my Father's looks. My whole life people have asked, "Where did you get that smile?" My response has always been, "I don't know! I'm adopted!" That had been my tag line for years.

Chapter 15

May 1, 2007

Happy Birthday to me! It's just another day at the casino. I will have a lovely evening when I get home with my family. I can't wait to get home. My Mom and Dad called and wished me a wonderful day. My kids and friends called too. I wondered if my birth Mom would give me a call. I know my birth Dad was sending kisses from heaven.

Mother's Day 2007

Fabulous day! I met my parents for brunch. I brought my Mom a gorgeous bouquet of flowers. She loves cut flowers like I do. It just brightens her day and she fusses over them for a week. I had to work at the casino afterwards and got to pass out orchids to all the Moms in my department. I came home to a lovely dinner and presents from my husband and kids.

I thought about my decision to search for my birth family. It has messed with my head a bit but given the chance again, yeah, I would do it.

Chapter 16

Wow, it's now 8/17/07. It's been a few months since I have added anything. I have been keeping in constant touch with Kalin. I have not heard from anyone else. Kalin had a great sense of humor and we were very much in sync. We haven't spoken on the phone because (I think) we're happy where our comfort level was. He told me another eerie coincidence, his parents adopted a daughter named Sheri, spelled Shari. She died of an overdose in her early 20s I believe.

When Kalin heard, my name was Sheri, he was taken back a little bit. Sarah (my daughter) had baby Evan on July 21st. He is such a wonderful part of our lives. I now know that I can love a grandchild as much as I love my own children. He is just one more miracle God has given us.

Anyway, I told Kalin, I would call him when the baby came. It took all I could muster up to make the call. We had been playing it so safe. No hesitation in phone conversations, just emails. So, I made the call and got his answering machine. I bumbled through a message telling him all about Evan. He emailed, apologized for missing my call and thought the call was cute. He appreciated it. He said he wanted to be part of Evan's life. That's all I needed. I had a new brother. I knew that for sure. It was such a cool feeling. And it was wonderful hearing his voice.

To back up a little bit, I sent an email Bill Medley's Manager in March. He said he was Bill's best friend and Bill didn't use a cell phone. He said he would be happy to give Bill my number and asked how I was doing. I told him I was a wonderfully grounded person with a husband and a beautiful life. Johnny said that made him feel good. He said that Bill would be in touch with me shortly.

That night, Bill called me and left a message. I was still at work. He said that he knew about me. He left his number to call me back. He said he was anxious and looking forward to meeting me. It was a very kind and warm message.

When I got off work, I pulled into a parking lot close by. I wasn't going to drive 45 minutes before I called him. Bill answered right away. He asked how I was and if I was okay. I thanked him for calling and explained that I was a very grounded person with a wonderful life. I was married with three beautiful children and one new grandbaby. I let him know that all was good in my life.

He then told me that he was going to be at South Point Casino in Las Vegas in a month or so and would love to get together. He said his daughter was going to be in town too so we could meet her also. That was a wonderful idea and I told Bill that I could probably make it happen. It was a great conversation and he made me feel at ease.

Bill finally asked me about my life up there and how I liked living in Washington. I told him that I loved it and we lived in a farmhouse on six acres. He said he agreed with how beautiful the Northwest was.

We talked for about 20 minutes. He asked a lot of questions about my life. Again, I told him that I was fine, and I had a great life. I don't think he realized I was adopted out. I believe he assumed my birth mother kept me. He said, "So you were adopted by a new family when you were six weeks?" I said, "Yeah, it was a blessing. I had the most wonderful parents who raised me." He was very thoughtful, and I appreciated that.

I hung up feeling good. He then called back 2 minutes later and said, "Hi Sheri, this is Bill again". Like a goofball I said, "Hi Bill again". He said, "If there's anything you need at all, please don't hesitate to call me." He said, "I mean it, anything at all". I told him I appreciated that and that I would try to restrain myself from calling him, ha, ha, ha. I looked forward to seeing him in May when he was at the South Point Casino performing. We said our goodbyes, again, and I drove home.

We were a week from going to Vegas and I was so excited! Had the hotel booked, the flight booked, the car rented and time off from work. Then I got an email and found out his show was cancelled. I was so looking forward to it! And just to get away. I called his friend Johnny and he told me that the show was cancelled because the showroom wasn't done. Man, that was a bummer. I had to cancel our flight and only got half the credit…small airport. Luckily, I was able to cancel our room and car with no additional fees.

We are going to see Bill and McKenna on August 24th. I made reservations at South Point Casino and Hotel. Now I am really ready for a vacation! I'm not the least concerned that it will be 100 degrees. Living in Washington, although beautiful, you just got to get out. Our summers are too short. Growing up in California, I was used to 9 months of summer like weather. As long as we can get out of here once in a while, I stay sane.

I don't know if I have mentioned this but since I found out who I was, obviously, I want to know all The Righteous Brothers music. Each paycheck I have bought a CD. Once I bought them all, I started buying the albums. I have a wonderful collection now and am amazed at the unbelievable talent of The Righteous Brothers!

I have SO many favorite songs like, "Stranded in the Middle of No Place", "Here I am", "Dream On", "Ebb Tide", "White Cliffs of Dover", "The Angels Listened In", "Is it so Wrong", "Hang Ups", "Soul Café", "Soul and Inspiration", "Just Once in my Life" along with "Unchained Melody". I could name a dozen more of my favorites but that is just off the top of my head.

And I should remember to mention, "You've Lost That Lovin' Feeling" which is the most played song in the history of American Radio. I could go on and on about so many wonderful songs, but I am sure most of the people reading this already know what I am talking about. I just felt the need to know my father's music. That is why I wanted to see Bill. He spent so many years with my birth Dad. Maybe he would be willing to share some stories with me. I hope we can spend time over a glass of wine, and I can just listen to him reminisce.

Chapter 17

August 30, 2007

Las Vegas was a blast! We enjoyed every bit of it. The weather was hot and wonderful! We brought our youngest son, Nick. We had a great pool to keep us cool every day. Pete and I went to Bill's show Friday night. We let Nick rent some video games, so he was a happy camper. I was completely pumped up and excited to hear the band. I was not a bit disappointed. They were spectacular!

The slide show caught me off guard. As Bill sang "Unchained Melody". I had never heard him sing is before. It was a mellow, toned-down rendition of Bobby's song. While he was singing, a wonderful slide show of Bobby Hatfield was displayed. There were so many pictures I had never seen before. I was overcome. I don't know how else to describe it. Pete knew how I felt because he was probably choked up himself. Pete just rubbed my back in silence. He knew how much this had gotten to me. This show continued with laughs and wonderful songs. It lifted all of our spirits. Bill had a good thing going and the best thing by far, in my humble opinion, was that slide show.

Once the show ended, we waited in line to see Bill afterward. While we were in line, Bill's wife Paula, came up to me and introduced herself. She was lovely. She said, "Sheri, as hard as it was for me to watch the show including the slide show, I could only imagine how you felt". She knew. She gave me a hug. That was very thoughtful, thank you Paula. I won't ever forget her words.

After we said our goodbyes and thanks to Paula, I couldn't help but notice, a couple behind us who had big smiles on their faces. I'm sure they heard our conversation. They looked like they are trying to strike up a conversation. Pete jumped in and said that I was Bobby Hatfield's daughter. It felt terrific to hear that. They introduced themselves as Marilyn and David. They looked a little star struck while looking at me. That was something new. Ha, ha. We talked for a while as we waited in line to see Bill. We briefed them on how I found out who I was. They thought it was pretty dang cool! We exchanged emails and I said we'd be in touch. We are dear friends to this day.

We met Bill's daughter McKenna first. She was sitting toward the beginning of the line. She was lovely and we exchanged kind words. I complimented her singing. She really belted out "At Last" and got a standing ovation.

Then it was time to meet Bill. He recognized me before I could say who I was. He gave me a big bear hug and asked how

I was doing. I thanked him for a fabulous show and said we needed to head back to our room to check on our 15-year-old son, Nick. When he heard that we brought our son with us, he gave us passes at his special table so we could go again the next night and bring Nick with us. You were supposed to be 21 but he said it would be okay and gave a wink. Nick was thrilled when we told him the news. These last few months, we hadn't been able to get away from The Righteous Brothers constantly playing in the house, lol, so he knew the music.

The second night we were seated at Bill's special table and didn't realize we were sitting with part of his old band, including Lee Ferrell and Richard Torres.

It was another fabulous show. I am super glad that I saw it twice because the first night felt like a blur. When the slideshow came on, it got to me again. I warned Nicky that the slideshow made me cry. Nicky just patted by back, not knowing what else to do. He was so sweet. I don't even know how he knew I was teary, but he was warned.

It was Lee Farrell's birthday and Bill acknowledged his presence along with a couple of other people in the audience. This might sound crazy, but I actually thought he was going to acknowledge me. It got me very nervous. Was I ready to be acknowledged? I was a jumble of nerves. The introductions ended and I was still the unknown birth daughter of Bobby Hatfield. I was okay with that.

We introduced ourselves to Richard and Lee after the show at my table. They were very nice, and I could feel the love they had for my Father. They shared several Bobby compliments. Richard looked at me pretty closely. Then he gave me a huge smile and a tap on the shoulder. I think he saw Bobby.

Once again, we waited in line to see Bill and McKenna. When we made it to the front of the line, I introduced Nick to Bill and McKenna. They both swooped in with big bear hugs. We took some pictures, and we were on our way. I believe he was celebrating Lee's birthday afterwards. I am disappointed that I couldn't have a glass of wine or a cup of coffee with him just to find out an extra something about my Dad, but that's okay.

He did check on me a couple of times when we were at the South Point Hotel/Casino. We were going out and about and I told him not to worry about us. We had a lot of adventures to go on. I'm sure he was glad that I wasn't just sitting around waiting and hoping for a Moment with him. We just had a wonderful rest of a vacation, Pete, Nick and I. Thank you, Bill.

Chapter **18**

It's now November 7, 2007. I really need to write more often. November 5th had been a bit emotional. I felt sad for the Hatfield family and for me. Bobby died so young. I just sent hugs to Kalin and let it go at that. He sent them back to me. I felt such a pit in my stomach, but did I have the right? Yes? No?

A couple of months ago, Kalin went to his Aunt Jeanne's for the weekend. He told her all about me. She was so excited! She then called me again and asked me a million questions. She told me it sounded like I was very grounded. I am. She said I was better off being raised AS I was.

Anyway, she said that she and Kalin would like to come up sometime or would love to have us down there. I gave her my MySpace address so she could see pictures. She's didn't do computers but her son, Clayton, was over it and he looked me up. I gave her the ages and birth dates of my family. I then received a lovely note from her.

Aunt Jeanne called yesterday, and we talked for about 30 minutes. She sounded so terrific. She filled me in a little more on the family. Then she said that Clayton just came over, so they sent me a lot of pictures. I was still at work, so I sat in my office and cried. My two uncles, I finally saw their faces. Both very handsome men, both have passed away. And Aunt Jeanne, you could just see her personality busting out. It was so wonderful to put faces with names. I have more family!

Clayton sent me a nice note and said he looked forward to meeting me. Man, that was a good feeling. It's been a year and after all this time, I thought it was only going to be Kalin who had accepted me. Now I had more family.

I had to stop for a minute because the phone rang. It was my Mom. She just wanted to say hi while Dad was at his Doctor's appt. I felt guilty about keep all this from them, but they truly did not want me to know anything about my birth family. Actually, my Dad would have been good with it. It was my Mom that was adamantly against it. At some point, I may have to tell them. But for now, it's better left unsaid.

A couple of months ago, I talked my parents about having Cherokee blood and I would have to get my original birth certificate to see if I had enough blood to be recognized. I worked at an Indian casino and my Dad actually brought it up in the first place. He said it may help me have better job security. My Mom said that it could open up a whole new can of worms. No, not worms, loving real people that shared the same ancestry as I did.

I think we're going to try and fly down to Palm Dessert after the holidays, maybe late January or February. I didn't know who all wanted to meet me, but I did know that it would be wonderful no matter what!

Chapter 19

Valentine's Day 2008

I have a sister named Vallyn, who was born on Valentine's Day. She is the same age as my oldest son Brandon. Happy Birthday little sister.

April 4, 2008

Things are going along at a slow but at a good pace. We had a great holiday. Having baby Evan brought magic back to Christmas. It was a whole new dynamic having a child around at Christmas. Magic came back into our house. What a great and wonderful time!

I got a card from Kalin, so I finally know what his girlfriend looks like. One day in December he sent me an email and said that he proposed to Nikki on the Price is Right during a station break. What? Hahaha!

He said that Drew Carey gave them a shout out and they might be on TV. So, on February 11th, with the TV recording, we watched. And toward the end, Drew Carey introduced Kalin and Nikki. It was very cool. It's so nice to see him in 3D rather than in pictures. I think I watched it about 10 times, no exaggeration.

At the casino, I have always been in charge of the annual New Year's Eve party for all the elite Players (whales). It was a lot of work, but so unbelievably successful. People talked about it for weeks. I received several bottles of wine and a number of hand-written cards. One of the perks of the job, heehee. I have a High-End Slot Tournament coming up in June but for now, it's just nice to chill. Being a Slot Manager, I still have to schedule 42 people each week along with dealing with daily issues. There are many issues with employees, but nothing we can't overcome.

Chapter 20

One of the friends I have met and become friends with on MySpace is Larry Hanson. He played with Alabama for 18 years and also with The Righteous Brothers for a few years before that. He thought the world of Bobby and has told me some very nice things about him. He has never hesitated to answer any questions, silly or not. I will always be grateful for his friendship. He is one of the kindest and gentlest souls I have ever met.

About a week ago he told me about a MySpace page that was about when the Righteous Brothers were Bobby Hatfield and Jimmy Walker. He thought I'd enjoy it, which I did.

They produced one album together (which I obtained through good ole eBay) called Re-Birth. It was wonderful to see a couple of pictures I hadn't seen before. And believe me; if they are on the internet, I've seen almost all of them!

I decided to send a note to the person who put together the MySpace page. I asked if it was Jimmy Walker. I said if it was, he knew my Dad. I received an email back saying that she was a good friend of Jimmy Walker's and who was my Dad.

I answered her by saying Bobby Hatfield was my birth Dad. I told her that I have only known for about a year and a half and was taking things real slow by getting to know the family etc. I said that I would appreciate it if she kept things between us.

She answered by saying, "I didn't expect you to say Bobby Hatfield! He was so famous and what a legend!" She wanted to know details and for some reason I felt compelled to tell her. I got feelings about people sometimes and this felt okay. I know I've mentioned this before. She told me that she interviewed Jimmy in 2005 and they became good friends and just hit it off. She said they emailed and phone each other quite often. She was French but had lived in England for many years. She then said her partner of 14 years was Chris Dreja of The Yardbirds. She asked if I knew of them. I thought of the song, "For your Love". I'm sure there are many more that I have heard of.

I gave her the short version of how I found out that Bobby Hatfield was my birth Father. When my husband got home, I told him about the MySpace page and about my corresponding with a lady named Katy from England. I said she lived with Chris Dreja who is the drummer for The Yardbirds. My husband immediately perked up and said, "Do you know the history of The Yardbirds Sheri?" Evidently, I didn't. He told me about how Eric Clapton, Jimmy Page and Jeff Beck came from that original band. He got out his History of Rock book and looked up The Yardbirds. So that was fun for him. I told Katy about that and she loved it.

This happened two days ago, and I will write more when I hear back from her. It will be interesting to communicate with Jimmy Walker if he chooses to contact me. It's really kind of incredible...this whole thing. It still feels more like a story than a reality. Once I meet some of the family, I think I will be more at ease. He was my Father and I know he's looking down on me with acknowledgement and love.

Chapter 21

April 11, 2008

Katy and I had been emailing back and forth that last week. She had filled me in on things and I have told her more of my story. She was keeping my story in confidence but was so very fascinated by the whole thing. Love you Katy. She said I should ask Reno Bellamy to be my friend. He was cousins with Barry Rillera and he and Bobby were so close for so many years. I thanked her and was excited to learn more about my birth Father.

I went ahead and requested Reno as a friend on MySpace. He accepted right away and sent the nicest comment. I was very touched. It said, "Sheri, thank you so much for the request. I like your page and your family pics. See you're a big fan of Billy and Bobby's. We grew up together. Honor is all mine." Then he sent a picture of himself and Bonnie Tyler after a concert in Montreal. What a nice thing to say. I decided to tell him who I was. I kept it brief.

He emailed right back and said, "I knew there was something special about you. Well you probably already know Johnny Lopez (Uncle) Barry and Butch Rillera and Jose Silva (my cousins) with my older brother Tony (T-Bone) of Redbone was the first band for them in high school. They used to practice at my Mom's restaurant in Santa Ana. (Wow, what incredible information. "Come and Get Your Love" was one of my all-time favorite songs. Wow!) Your dad tried to get me to coach his son's football but I was too busy at the time".

(I was fascinated by his words. What a great guy.) "Let me know when you're ever in Vegas. It would be great to meet you and your husband. You're family now. P.S. They use to call me Rennie".

I truly love Reno! Just like that he accepted me.

How much more incredible could that email be? "You're family now". I WAS FAMILY NOW. I had no idea how those words would make me feel. I waited almost a year and a half to hear that. He accepted me just like that...no hesitation. Well needless to say, it made me cry. I have a family that I love very deeply. But I also have a whole other side that I am meant to know. Everything happens for a reason and I have been very patient trying not to push myself on the family. I just wish it was as easy as it was with Reno.

I knew that Kalin and Aunt Jeanne and the cousins all accepted me, but the other siblings for some reason weren't as receptive. I really shouldn't have said that. It sounded like I was whining. I just didn't know what my other siblings were

65

thinking. I wished they would have just told me. I understood Bobby Jr. and how he was content with his life as it was. That was fine. But the others. It made my mind wander and the insecurities set in. I knew that they had thought about if I had expected any financial gain. I probably would have wondered the same thing too if my Father was a legend. I have not searched for financial gain. I made a very comfortable living. I had no rights to any of the Hatfield money. I had searched for my blood, my family, my looks. That was it!

Maybe I'll never really know why. Hopefully someday, they will all have accepted me. If they don't, I am still blessed with new friends and family. I made the right decision; I just knew it. I still had a best family ever. I was good.

I emailed Reno back and thanked for being so gracious and said I would love to meet him someday. I knew it would happen. I was able to get a good night's sleep and didn't think or dream about my adoption at all.

Two days ago, I got another email from Reno. He said, "Sheri, on the 4th of July, in the city of Corona, we're doing a concert. The band was hand-picked by Johnny Lopez. It included Barry Rillera, Larry Hanson, maybe Jose if he's in town, me and my sister, Michaelina. I will forward you all the info when I get it all. Everyone grew up with your Dad. It might be a good chance to meet everyone. P.S. They too will accept you and your family. Your look is his. LOL Reno."

How's a person supposed to sleep after getting an invitation like that? We always had a 4th of July party, but I think we'll have to change it to 5th of July. I've just got to make it down there. What a wonderful opportunity to meet everyone, especially Reno. What a special man. My wheels are spinning, and I have got to figure things out. I think I have enough Alaska air miles. I will have to see what Kalin and Aunt Jeanne are up to that week. I hope to see them and then finish up with the concert. This whole thing is incredible. Have I said that a thousand times before yet? Go to sleep Sheri.

My morning came with a jolt. I had to get ready for work now. I had to be at the casino by 2 pm. Yesterday I was just walking around with a dumb smile on my face. I'll probably do the same today. I wish my family could go with me to the concert, but we're going to Hawaii in August and saving pennies. My husband has been so supportive and agreed that I needed to go. That means yes, I have decided to take the next step. I plan to meet my birth family!

Pete and Nick are planning to go down to our niece's wedding in Sacramento. All his family will be there from Florida. It will be wonderful for them. Wish I could be there too, but it was at the same time as my concert. My husband has been a rock through this whole process for me.

Chapter 22

April 13, 2008

I have still been walking in a cloud about the whole acceptance thing. I asked Bertie Higgins to be my friend on MySpace because I saw that he was a friend of Reno's. I can't even remember if I have mentioned that for some reason, certain songs make me cry. I've never really understood why. Is it because they were touching or romantic? Most likely. I am so corny, it's actually quite embarrassing at how easily I cry. Aunt Jeanne said that Bobby was the same way. She said he'd cry at the simplest things. Could I relate to that or what?

I clicked on Bertie's site. I had no idea he wrote and recorded Key Largo. How did I not know that? Oh, my gosh, that was one of the songs that I couldn't help but cry. Wow. Also, one of my all-time favorite songs is "Back to the Island" again by Bertie. As I was listening to his beautiful voice, I decide to check out his friends. Holy! I am there in his top 40 out of about 500. Reno must have told him about me. Yay! I felt like the daughter of Bobby Hatfield. That was nice of Bertie.

I checked out my mail and there was an email from Larry Hanson. He said he was definitely was going to play in Corona, California. He said that everyone would welcome me with open arms just as he would. He said he would love to meet me. He explained that he was on tour for 10 shows with his daughter Jennifer Hanson, an amazing country singer. She was gorgeous, could sing and was a songwriter. Larry shared that she actually wrote another of my favorites performed by The Wrecking Crew, "Leave the Pieces When You Go". I felt like I was living it a dream and was going to wake up soon.

He was so proud of her, as he should be. Between you and me right now, I sure wish I was gifted with a beautiful voice. It wasn't as God intended, but I had been singing all of my life and way before The Voice came on, I would close my eyes during American Idol. I usually picked the top 2. I had an ear for music and still do.

I know that this was a very special time in my life. I had to embrace what was accepted and not worry about what was not. I had a fabulous family. Anyone else would be so totally blessed to hook up with us. I was famous in my own little world and what a wonderful world it was!

But I am excited about my adventure south. I really wish I could head down with Pete and Nick, but we just can't afford it. We're saving up for Kauai in August. And I have to be brutally honest. I would give up Kauai in a New York second just to spend more time down with Bobby's old buddies. Of course, the family would have to be with me. But we've already paid for our condo. I have to realize that going to Hawaii is a phenomenal vacation and we have been lucky enough to go a few times. These new friends of mine have accepted me and will welcome me whenever I can visit.

Chapter **23**

May 31, 2008

Well, I did it!! It took me about six weeks to call Aunt Jeanne and commit to come down. She said I could stay with her and she'd drive me everywhere. Why did it take me so long to make that one call? She is the best thing ever and probably always has been.

I emailed Kalin and he said he didn't have any plans for the first week of July. He said he was really excited and would love if I came down! He said that he and Nikki could come to Palm Springs and hang with me for the weekend if it was alright with me. I emailed back, "Are you kidding me? I'm coming down mainly for you!"

To backtrack, Pete, Nick and my oldest son Brandon ended up going to Sacramento. They had a great time! The east coast (Florida) family on my husband's side was there and it was truly wonderful. All blood relatives. My kids have been my only blood relatives. I had a feeling it was going to be another sleepless night!

Now back to Aunt Jeanne. I told her that I wanted to come down the first week of July. She was so excited! She said she didn't have any plans. She asked me to stay with her. I accepted her generous offer. Wow, just like that, she accepted me and trusted me to stay with her.

I really can't imagine what to expect. Throughout this journey almost every time I have shared my story, I have either brought tears to people's eyes or they have said, "I have never heard such a wonderful story, you should write a book!" I hope that I have relayed my story well enough for you to embrace the emotions that I have been through. And I am talking about dozens and dozens of people telling me this, not one or two. Even the Director I work for said, "Hell, I'd buy the book!" This has turned into a very unique and fabulous journey so far.

Two dear couples I met at my Casino are Lloyd and Jo-Anne and Dick and Joanne. When I told them what I found out about my birth family, tears just rolled down their eyes. They made sure I updated them weekly. They almost couldn't wait to see me. They felt the incredible story unfolding and felt very protective also. I am blessed to have had these people in my life.

I emailed Kalin and told him that Aunt Jeanne was available that week. I asked him if he would go to the concert in Corona with me (and his fiancé). He said he would check and get back with me. I didn't tell Aunt Jeanne about it yet because I won't go if they don't want to go. That was on July 4th, on a Friday night at a park called Santana Park.

All of this happened on Friday while I was at work. I hadn't told Pete that it was a done deal. I happened to have enough Alaska Miles that the trip is only costing me $7.50. Score!

When I told Pete, he was happy for me and yet wasn't comfortable with me going down there alone. He is feeling a bit leery, which I understand. We don't do much traveling apart. But I think this will be good this time. He's very protective but I don't think he needs to worry. I have only travelled without him when I go to my high school reunions. I always go with my best friend Pammy. This will be my first flight flying solo, but it is all good. I can look through my photo album. I put together pictures of my family and home. I also brought all of the side-by-side pictures of Bobby and I. I also brought my adoption information in case anyone one was curious about that.

When I made the decision to meet the family, I seriously got dry mouth, my heart palpitated, and my hands were shaking. I really don't know how Aunt Jeanne deciphered my message. But it has been a year and a half in the making. I have gotten to know Kalin so well that I really do believe that I love him. He's been a wonderful guy that has always accepted me and yet has been honest and curious. He has truly been a loving brother from the start. Not judging me or wondering if I was really after something else. Thank you, Kalin.

It's now June 20th and I have been planning to call Aunt Jeanne all week. She sounds absolutely wonderful, honest and open. Why was it so hard for me to call? I did find out from Kalin that he can't make the concert because his best friend was in town and he had made plans with his family. He also said that he had an issue with one of the original RBs but I would let that go. My reason for wanting to go to the concert is to see Reno and Larry. Hopefully Aunt Jeanne will want to go with me. Fingers crossed.

Chapter 24

My Mom and Dad thought I was going to a work-related conference. I really hated to BE deceiving them, but I knew it is better that way. My Mom really, really never wanted me to make contact. I understood her views. I was hers. I respected her wishes all these years and if the non-id hadn't been so personal, I still wouldn't have.

I believe that things happened for a reason and this was meant to be. How could she think I would love my birth parents more than her and Dad? They have been the only parents I have ever known, and I hit the jackpot with them. It was a match made in heaven. I am not saying that my life was perfect, or I didn't have challenges as I grew up. But I can actually say that I wouldn't have changed it for the world.

I haven't told my brothers either. I think that they might have felt compelled to tell my parents. I didn't believe is was for spite, but perhaps they would have felt a responsibility, I guess. There will probably come a time that I will share my story with them, certainly before this book gets published, if it gets published. I guess if you're reading this then woo hoo, I did it! Wow, that was a pretty wonderful thing to dream about.

Okay, back to my journey.

It is now just 10 short days before I meet my family, I have been getting butterflies. Lots and lots of butterflies. I have been wondering how I would be feeling when I finally got to meet my birth family. I thought about is for a while. I had no idea.

I know it would be good though. I'm about 10 pounds overweight and 50 years old! Who cares? Why would that bother them? I had been running almost every day to try and stay in shape, but where did this gut come from? I have never had a thick stomach in my life! I guess that's where the age 50 comes in. Yay for me.

At least that was the only symptom I was dealing with. My friends talked about hot flashes, sounds horrible. My girlfriend actually had a little battery-operated fan. She pulled it out when we were having lunch a little while ago. Ha, ha, ha! That was so funny! She said, "Just you wait!" Got to love my Debra. And Nancy too. She was dealing with the dreaded hot flash.

I still don't know who all I'm going to meet down there. I know for sure Aunt Jeanne, her kids and families, Kalin and his fiancé and maybe Vallyn. Kalin had been filling me in as time went on.

I was aware that is was totally up to them if they want to get to know me. I think Bobby Jr. was happy with his life and didn't need anything else. That was okay. I needed to stop dwelling on what I could not have and just be thankful for what I did have.

As many emotions as I have felt over that last year and a half, I was still glad finally know my heritage and who I was. I have cried countless times, felt hurt, mad, scared, abandoned, sad, confused, worried and empty. But I have also felt elated, overjoyed, loved, intrigued, satisfied and truly happy. I would always recommend to everyone to find your roots.

Even though my birth Mom has decided not to get to know me, I still know my roots. I know where my oldest son gets his black hair and striking blue eyes.

I have a girlfriend who told me she found out she was adopted a couple months ago. She told me who her Father is and he was a famous country singer. I have been sworn to secrecy and will respect her wishes. I can't talk her in to finding him. She didn't want to be rejected. I told her to just write him a letter stating she doesn't want his money and wasn't asking for anything. She needed to let him know she existed. Her mother never told him. She only found out a few months back when her adopted Father was on his death bed. They kept it a secret her whole life. Why? I still don't understand why people don't get that the more you have to love, the better. The is no way to have too many people to love.

I knew this man would love to know he had a beautiful daughter out there just as I know Bobby Hatfield would have loved me. She's lucky because he was still alive. I don't know if I will ever be able to talk her into it. You have to follow the path that was right for you, but dang what could a letter hurt? He seemed like a lovely man and she had his exact same smile.

I am going to close for now. I have to get my run in with the dogs before getting ready for work. My next entry will be AFTER I talk with Aunt Jeanne. I'm such a chicken!

Chapter 25

June 26, 2008

What was my problem? Aunt Jeanne was so accepting and wonderful. She was so excited to talk with me and even more excited that I was coming down. I told her all about the concert and how many of Bobby's old friends were going to be there and I had hoped that she might want to go with me. Aunt Jeanne answered like it was no big deal, "Sure, we'll plan on it." I think I might have thanked her a dozen times but then we had a great conversation and made plans for when I came down. She said she had everything under control. I had no doubts. Now all I had to do was just sit back and enjoy the ride.

I know that I will have Kalin and Aunt Jeanne in my life for the rest of my days. I can't wait for them to meet my husband and children and beautiful grand baby Evan. I haven't felt this happy in a long time. I can't explain the joy of getting to know my birth family.

If I haven't said this 100 times before, things are meant for a reason. Karma is real. I was meant to find my birth family. There are so many truly weird things that have brought this all together.

I guess I am at a pivotal point in my life. Introduce the Hatfield family. They are the people I look like and perhaps act like. What an unbelievable feeling to meet my blood relatives for the first time. To actually have the same smile or chin or an inflection when we talk would be just amazing. When I saw Bobby Hatfield do that "shimmy" when singing Unchained Melody, I had to show my friends at work and they both almost got weirded out. They also got teary. When I get excited about something I do, "the shimmy".

When they saw the video, they both said, "Okay no more, that's too much!!!"

Now I have found out that I had blood relatives that wanted to meet me, it was an unbelievable feeling. I was flying out in 5 days to meet family who were going to welcoming me with open arms. Who did that? Maybe this is happening all over the world, but it is so new to me. In the same breath, it doesn't mean that I have any less love for my beautiful family that I grew up with. I love my parents and my brothers. That will never change. I am sure I probably didn't even need to throw this comment in.

There is no limit to love. The more you have, the more you give. If you don't know what I mean about this then we have to talk. It doesn't matter how much you own, or what you have but it is about how much you are blessed with loved ones. My whole life, I was always working on family reunions. I was successful in several. I even sent out all of the invitations and helped prepare all of the food during the reunions, just so we could be together. I grew up with one 2nd cousin, Brian Kaylor, who was my age. His sisters were 3-4 years older, so it was always us. I loved him and he was still #1 in my heart to this day. We live a couple of states away from each other now. I treasure every moment we spent together. And one great memory was him driving the golf cart around the neighborhood and he was only 14! Good one Brian!

Luckily, our kids grew up together and when we moved up north, we would always meet at the halfway point (McDonalds) so our kids could spend weekends together. I know our kids made tons of wonderful memories and videos that they could share but would probably die of embarrassment first.

I still do have this lingering guilt about not letting my parents know that I have contacted my birth family. My Mom was in an auto accident when she was 18 and after a long hospital stay, she was told that she would not be able to bear any children. I know that I was meant to be their daughter and what a great childhood I had.

I have always known that I was adopted. My parents always told me that many families had babies, but I was chosen and very special. I was told that when they laid me in the arms of my parents, everything fit into place perfectly." And I went home to my new family.

Chapter 26

I spent most of the years of my life NOT trying to find my roots. I had wonderful parents and felt like I lived a charmed life. I had a family of my own and so much going on. My parents never asked if I wanted to find my birth family. I know they never wanted me to find my birth family.

Now I get back to why I originally started this journal. I needed to know if I had heart disease in the family, or high blood pressure or cancer or what?

I am a woman who has been married almost 29 years. I had had a few blood-pressure checks that have been a bit higher than I had expected. I never pig out...19 out of 20 times, I always ate healthy. I ran at least mile or two and race walk the third mile. Why in the world would I have high blood pressure? It wasn't scary high, but I'll bet I could fix it by exercising more.

I just remembered an old conversation. My Mom and my grandmother said, "Never get old!" I heard that about a thousand times. I told them I would try not to and we all laughed because we knew it was the future that God gave us. Because of all of those conversations, I'd checking my blood pressure more often to make sure I was all good.

It's time to say good night for now. I will go to bed with such anticipation of my trip next week. I am finally going to meet my wonderful brother Kalin, a Godsend named Aunt Jeanne, and whoever else was in the cards. I knew that my life would be richer, and I would have more love from my new family, and it was a truly indescribable feeling

June 27, 2008.

What a day! I don't know when I'll be able to go to sleep. I got an email from Kalin today. He was wondering if I'd be interested in coming to a BBQ at his house on Thursday, if that was okay. Are you kidding me? He said that he invited Bobby and Kristen and the boys. My heart about fell to the floor. Is Bobby really going to come and meet me? I haven't heard from him since the first-time Pete contacted him.

Are things really falling into place and was there going to be a reunion that was beyond my dreams? Kalin also said that he invited Vallyn. I was feeling overwhelmed, again, but I couldn't have asked for anything more. I realized now that I was going to have to just take things as they came. I had to just be grateful for whatever came my way. But my little nephew who was the spitting image of me when I was 5, was going to be there.

I am so worried about what they will think of me. I'm not worried about Aunt Jeanne or Kalin. But Bobby and Vallyn really don't know anything about me. My friends say, "Just be yourself and they will naturally fall in love with you." I want to believe them and I know they are right but I still have the insecurities that are coming out of nowhere. I really should be on track with this but here are some people that have known about me for a year and a half, but still don't know me. I could just totally go on and on but why? It's all going to work out beautifully.

I got an email today from Bertie Higgins. He sent me a video of Reno playing Tonga's.

It was on YouTube called Superstars Latinos. It was great and I got to see Reno in action. I put in on my MySpace. Very cool.

So yeah, I'm pretty much living the dream. I have been so in love with music all my life and now will be meeting people who have made a living through music, incredible. I wish my husband and family could be with me on my trip next week, but I'm just grateful that it has happened.

Really, things are working out so wonderfully. It has been a year and a half since I found out Bobby Hatfield was my Father. When I found out who he was…I was floored. But then I was devastated that I waited so long to find him. I have researched the Righteous Brothers for so long now and have read so many tender loving comments about Bobby. I believe that I do love my birth Father, although I never met him. The more I learn, the better I feel. I also know he was not an Angel, ha!

Chapter 27

June 29, 2008

Another day has passed. I heard again from Kalin. He was still very excited about the BBQ. I found out that he had talked to Bobby's wife Kristen and she was excited about it all. Hopefully she'll talk Bobby into coming. I sure would like to meet my nephews. I'll have to explain that I'm the "older" Aunt but truly the coolest. Ha! Kalin also hasn't heard back from Vallyn yet, but however it works out, it's all good.

I got an email today from a friend who I met through a girl that I work with. She told her about my story. She had a husband who was adopted and wanted to find his birth family. I put them in touch with the search angels I knew and he had already met his birth Mom and the extended family. It was an elated Moment, although humbling feeling, that I had a part in it. I know that I will volunteer in the future to help reunions as soon as the time is right. I have helped a second couple, but she's not quite ready to call her brother. All in good time. To each his own.

Anyway, she told me about how this guy came into her work and wanted a gift certificate for his "birth sister". How great is that? She had to dig further and found out it was the same group that I put her in touch with. That was such a warm, satisfying feeling in the heart. I belong to a group called NWASR in Washington State. Ironically it turns out that the search angel that found my family out of California, is an active member of this group. They are very special people. They have changed my life forever.

Karma is around every corner and if people don't believe that things happen for a reason, well they are probably very short sided and can't quite grasp the thought of an afterlife. I know that one of the reasons that I try to be the best person I can be each and every day is to reunite with my daughter, Krissy, who passed away when she was only 4 ½. Why wouldn't I do my best? She's the angel that guides me.

Since I brought up Krissy, I think I will speak of her just for a short bit. She died of SUDS...sudden unexplained death syndrome. Kind of like SIDS but in an older child. How do you possibly get a handle on that?

I cannot let you know about this horrific time in my life but I will tell you that she had old photo books opened to pages of our relatives that have passed. I believe she was letting us know that these wonderful relatives have come to get her and that she is fine. It was eerie, soothing, confusing all at the same time. I don't believe I will ever get over her death, nor will I ever be as happy as I was when she was alive. Even writing this has brought me to tears.

Now I will share a miracle that was given to us. Pete had a vasectomy after we had our 3 children. After Krissy died, we waited a year and decided that Pete should have a reversal. We made the appointment. Since it was elective, insurance was out of the picture. We went to Seattle and the procedure was done.

As many people I assume wonder, we did not decide to have another baby to replace our beautiful angel. But we did try to heal our family. We had 5 and 7-year-old children that were in such deep sorrow. I got pregnant and can still remember coming out to our bed where Pete, Brandon, Sarah and I were watching TV in the bedroom before nite-nite time. I said the test was positive and that they were going to have a little brother or sister. It brought hope back into our lives.

As a mother of 34, I did very well. I got a couple of funky spider veins on my inner knee which ticked me off. Ah, the small price you pay.

I went into labor and the baby was early. I went into labor the day before my beautiful Krissy passed away two years ago. This left a panic in all of my friends and family, praying that I would give birth that day. They were trying to figure out how to handle it if the baby for born on Krissy's death day.

I gave birth to Nicholas Benton Strobaugh at 5:15 pm at night. I had a long labor, which is unusual, since it was my fourth child.

My husband and Mom were in the room when I gave birth. I was so exhausted because of the long labor. I was glad they were there to enjoy him, our little miracle.

Chapter 28

Nicholas made some hard-exhaling sounds…a bit labored. After a couple of minutes, the nurses decided to whisk him away. They took him out of my arms and said they needed to run a test and not to worry. Where are they taking him?

Fifteen minutes later I was at the delivery table all by myself. I hadn't been cleaned up and no one was around. No husband, no Mom, no doctor, no nurse, no baby. I got up and walked out of the room across to the bathroom in the hall. I saw my husband and parents all huddled up with the Doctor down the hall.

I was so exhausted from my 12-hour labor that it was even hard to walk across the hall, just to use the bathroom. My family knew I saw them. What in the world was going on! Where was my baby and why did everyone leave me alone? Everyone came back into the room when I finished my potty run. The Doctor said that Nicholas's lungs were not fully developed. He had one shot of medication to help soften the tissue in his lungs. Since he was a preemie, he needed special care. That was when they told me I wouldn't be holding my baby. I didn't understand. They Doctor assured me that he was going to be all right, but he needed to be down at The Children's Hospital in Seattle. I was informed that my son was going to be helicoptered to the NICU at Children's Hospital.

I was living in another nightmare and can't believe this was happening to me. My baby was getting flown out of here and I could not go with him. I had to keep the faith and know that my baby was going to be all right.

At 4:30 am I listened as my baby was helicoptered away from me and there was nothing I could do. Everyone was sleeping around me, but I heard the helicopter fade in the distance. What an absolutely sickening feeling. I would never forget that helpless, empty and horrific feeling. My husband and daughter were sound asleep, and I wasn't going to share my sorrow. I would not have been able to explain my sorrow and I was grateful that they were sleeping peacefully instead of feeling what I was going through. I will never forget the sound of the helicopter flying away knowing my son was in it. I was not allowed to leave until I was released. I had to be there at least 12 hours. Didn't they understand what that does to a mother? I wept silent tears for a countless amount of time.

They released me in the morning, and we drove directly down to Seattle to see our baby. My oldest, Brandon, was staying at a friend's house. I had filled them in and they would care for Brandon until we got home. He was 10 and I wanted all of the information before letting Brandon know what was going on.

When we arrived at the hospital, we found out that he was the sickest little baby in the entire ward. We needed to keep have faith. They had to bring him back twice. When I heard that, I thought I would die myself. We spent the next 12 days going to the hospital and being by his side. The kids were troopers and went with us every day.

After 12 days in the ICU, Nicholas went from the sickest baby to the healthiest baby in the ward. What a fabulous miracle! Thank you, God!

I never slept through the night without checking on Nicky. After he made through 4 ½ years of life, I started sleeping through the night.

And that was probably more than I should have shared but this was part of an incredible circumstance. If you knew anything about childbirth, then you knew that the mother really needs a couple of weeks to recuperate from the birth. I didn't have any symptoms or pain while my little baby was in the ICU, I was like on hold. I needed to focus on my child. I didn't have to deal with any of that until my baby was home safe with me. How can you not believe in God after that? I have a miracle child, plain and simple.

Chapter 29

And if you were wondering what this had to do with my whole adoption story? Well, that little miracle son of mine has the same exact lips, jawline and smile as Bobby Hatfield, his grandfather. It thoroughly gave me chills the first time I realized it.

I haven't shared my emotions before and trust me, there were tons more! I felt compelled to share my story because I know there are so many parents of preemies that have been through similar stuff. Not knowing if their child was going to survive. What a crummy part in my life, but we made it through, and Nick grew up to be a thriving, talented young man.

I'm actually surprised with myself that I shared that. It was such a scary part of our lives. I could never be more grateful to have had a marriage that had lasted through a child's death and almost another, although it did change us forever.

Lose a child, you never get over it. You just deal with it and try to make it through, one day at a time. I am thankful for the many blessings that God has given us. I just know that I was this pistol up in heaven saying, "Yeah, I can do it, give me a tough one on earth!" What was I thinking?

I figure, once I have forgiven, then it was time to move on. And that is the way I have chosen to lead my life.

I have shared much more than I ever thought I would, and I will decide if I will delete tomorrow. For now, it felt good to talk about.

I have known that I was adopted all my life. My parents never tried to hide that. They said that I was special, I was chosen. My mother was in a horrible auto accident before she was 19 and had to have a hysterectomy, which I had mentioned before. Luckily, they had the option of adoption. I feel with all my might that this was meant to be. It definitely had an important role in my life as I grew up. Perfect, loving, beautiful parents. I couldn't have asked for anyone better. I had so many wonderful memories growing up. I never really thought much about finding my birth parents. I had the perfect parents.

There was just-one-thing.

Chapter 30

I have always wanted to have someone who looked like me. That was the only quirk about being adopted. I siblings and I didn't have any inflections that sounded the same. We didn't have anything that would let a stranger know we were related. That didn't make me love my brothers any less. It was just something that I didn't have. I would hang with my friends and see the resemblances all of the time as I watched them interact with her families. I have to admit, I did yearn for that a little bit.

All my life I would here, "Where'd you get that smile?" Or "Where'd you get those eyes?" I just laughed it off and said, "I don't know. I'm adopted!" I have mentioned this before, but I was actually asked that over a thousand times throughout the years. Even my first boss at a Title Company asked where I got my smile.

Aunt Jeanne sent me a picture of my birth Grandparents and boy do I look like my Grandmother. I have her nose to a T!

Hopefully I will be able to add the pictures I want to in this book so you can see what I'm talking about.

June 30, 2008

I have my big VIP Slot Tournament today and I'm pretty nervous. Not about the tournament, but about everyone showing up. They have a chance to win $10k, but not everyone has etiquette even though they have money. It will be a long day. I probably won't get home until 11 pm but then tomorrow I fly to Palm Springs. It's finally happening.

I had a dream that I was on the phone with my birth Mom. We had a great conversation. She was kind and funny. I have a tattoo on the side of my stomach of a Plumeria, with my initials below. My daughter Sarah and I got them at the same time. We have (had, she's married now) the same initials. Anyways in my dream when I told her about it she was so excited and said she wanted to get the same one too. Dreams, crazy huh?

Chapter 31

I got an email from Reno yesterday. He said that there was going to be between 10 and 20 thousand people at the concert on Friday. He wanted to get me VIP parking. He said that they were going to be practicing in Newport Beach on Wednesday and maybe my Aunt could pick up the passes. This is just perfect. We will be in Newport on Wednesday. Things were really falling into place. I'll call him on Wednesday, and we meet up somewhere.

I know my trip was going to go so fast. But being away from my family for four days was a long time. I've never been away by myself for this long. Maybe an overnight at a conference or something, but not four nights away. Pete is such a protector. I wish he was going but it will be fine. I have so many things to be nervous about. I wish there was a pill to fix it but I'm afraid there is not.

I'm hoping to write my thoughts while I'm down there, maybe at the end of the day. I have read so many reunion stories, some bad but a lot good. I can't believe that it was actually happening to me. My brother Kalin seemed just as excited as I am. Same with Aunt Jeanne. It was just so indescribable.

We are not meeting Linda and Vallyn for lunch on Wednesday. I guess Linda is ill. She has Lupus. She's doing okay but has times when she is worn out. I know that it will be a lot more comfortable for Vallyn and I to meet at Kalin's.

Well, it's time to get ready for work. Until next week...

June 30, 2008

Hey, here I am again. I just got home from my VIP slot tournament. It turned out great! I had some no shows, but I just let some spouses get in on it. The funny thing is that one of our biggest player's husband won the $10,000.00! It was hilarious! It was a very exhausting day but very fulfilling.

I have been called blonde bombshell, lovingly, for most of my career. I never found it insulting. It was in good fun. But since finding out who I was I thought, "If you only knew that was my birth Father's nickname...well blonde bomber." For some of the elite players that I have gotten close to know my story. I had a few more of them in tears tonight over my anticipation. They truly care for me and I can't explain how that made me feel. A few of them said basically, "Let your stomach settle down. Your family will love you just as we do." I'm telling you that I have incredible support from such loving people. If all goes well, my friends up here will be right, and my family will fall in love with me.

Here's the question, how am I supposed to go to sleep tonight knowing that I am going to meet some of my birth family tomorrow? I think it's a complete possibility that I won't but hopefully I'm wrong. I guess I should try and call it a day. Wish me luck!

Part four

Hatfields-Here I Come

Chapter 32

It's now July 8, 2008. I had an incredible trip! I'm a bit teary eyed right now. I had written Larry Hanson and Reno Bellamy and thanked them for the terrific concert and making me feel so welcome. I think I'll just have to copy what these wonderful people said: From Reno:

You were the sweetheart we all thought you'd be, everyone loved you and we'll make time for your whole family soon. Sheri it's hard to put into words how we felt to see you., we all loved your Dad.

The honor was all ours. XOXOXOXXOXOXO Cindy and Reno and our extended family that you are a part of. Reno

I know I have cried a lot throughout this journey, but that included a lot of happy tears. These people all knew my dad and they were so kind and loving to me. From Larry:

Hey Sheri, I just don't have the words to tell you how wonderful it was to meet you on the 4th! I would have loved to have more time to chat but hopefully in the future we'll see each other again. Thanks so much for making the trip down... I know it must have been an emotional trip but a much-needed trip for you! We were all so happy to meet you and I think Reno said it best when he said that you are family!

I am so overwhelmed by the emotion that they felt. They weren't just being nice. They truly were as thrilled to meet me as I was them. Bobby Hatfield must have impacted for lives that I imagined, especially these friends. After all, they were friends for many years.

I am going to fill you in about my trip. Here's how it started. I made it to the airport, but it was not easy. I somehow merged to the right when I was supposed to go straight. I got back on the freeway, went north and turned around. Unfortunately, the exit was under construction and closed. Somehow after much maneuvering, I got my car dropped off.

But wait, there's more. I brought a small bag so I wouldn't have to check it. Sadly enough, I had hairspray. I read online that it could be up to 16 oz. Mine was only 14 oz. The checker looked at me and raised his eyebrows. I said, "Ta dah! It's only 14 oz can!" What I didn't read was that it was for checked baggage only. I ended up checking my bag. The checker guy was really nice and said he appreciated my smile and enthusiasm. He walked me to the check point. That was embarrassing!

The airline announced that the flight was delayed for 30 minutes. Darn it! Oh well, that's less of a layover in San

Francisco. My body was starting to relax a bit. I couldn't find my book, so I think I'll treat myself to a new one. It felt good just to sit. I needed to get something to eat soon, that had been the last thing on my mind. I'm glad I'm feeling hungry, not as nervous. It's going to be a great day!

Chapter 33

I had a great flight. I met a gal named Fran. Ironically enough, she and her boyfriend of 15 years booked entertainment in Palm Springs. They had Eddie Money coming to Marin County at a park. I told her I was going to see the Barry Rillera's All Star Band with Larry Hanson, Johnny Lopez, Reno Bellamy, Michaelina Bellamy etc.

We hit it off. She said she lived in Coeur'dAlene, Idaho, ½ the time and the other in Palm Springs. She wasn't planning on the coming down on the 4th but her honey wanted her there. She was in her mid-sixties and very cool.

After an hour of chatting, I told her who I was. She was fascinated. She had never met the Righteous Brothers. I pulled out my album which included my non-identification adoption papers, pictures of Bobby and me and pictures of the Hatfields and the Strobaughs. I gave her the short version of how it all came about and how I was meeting my family for the first time.

She said that it was the best story that she had heard in a very long time. She told me I should write a book!

Then she told me about being involved in Rally Car Racing. Her boyfriend loved it! She shared a story about how she made Richard (her boyfriend) build an extra strong cage for the car. It was a good thing that she did because one day it was muddy and one of their tires stuck in the mud. Then the car shot into the air and landed on top of a tree stump! It then teetered, rolled off, and continued to roll down a hill.

Fran knew when they stopped rolling, she was probably hurt her head because she couldn't see. She didn't know that her helmet had slid over her face. When Richard asked if she was okay and she said yes, he released her seat belt and she dropped 3 feet. She didn't know she was upside down. She then also realized that she could see.

We ended up eating dinner together. I told her that I would let her know how my story turned out. I then talked to Fran about my Aunt Jeanne and she was making arrangements for my trip.

Fran told me a story about how she found these great high heeled tennis shoes. She loved them so much that she bought 3 pairs, red, black and white. When she met Patty La Belle during a show that they had booked, the first thing that Patty said was, "What size do you wear?" She was staring at Fran's high heeled tennis shoes.

She said, "Size 6." Patty was disappointed but they hit it off from then on.

Fran said she hoped that I would keep in touch with her and that she would love to hear more of the story. I will be contacting her in the next few days. She's a terrific person and we met for a reason. We parted our ways with a hug. I think she would have liked to see me meet my birth family.

Chapter 34

Five minutes after we parted, I was sitting down waiting for my baggage and I saw this adorable woman with a big smile...Aunt Jeanne! Her arms were extended, and she was just as I thought she'd be. I need to elaborate just for a minute. If you have ever imagined having that perfect Aunt, well I got her. She's cute, adorable and bubbly. She said that Clayton was outside somewhere. She is really amazing. I really loved her already! We found Clayton, he loaded my bags, and we were on our way.

We were talking a mile a minute and in no-time we made it back to her place and she immediately got out her photo albums. It was so perfect and just the thing I wanted to do. I get teary eyed. I'm seeing family pictures of my Father. My heart really started to race a bit. These are my roots. I am a Hatfield.

Bobby was my Birth Dad and we really did look alike. I'm going to bed tonight after looking at all those albums. It is a wonderful feeling to find your roots. In my same breath, I love my adopted parents very deeply. They will always be my parents.

I will elaborate just for a moment. My adopted parents thought that I was at a conference in Palm Springs. It really was true...several conferences. But I didn't want them to worry about anything. They had too much going on. They never wanted me to search so hopefully they will never know what I have found.

Aunt Jeanne's condo was beautiful and decorated in a soft powder blue and her kitchen red and white. I felt very comfortable being there.

Aunt Jeanne gave me her bedroom and she slept on the couch. Wow, that made me feel so bad, but I know there's no talking her out of it. She said she loved her couch. That was just one small amount of what she was all about. She was only worrying about me. Aunt Jeanne, I love you so much! You truly are one of a kind.

Before we went to bed, I looked over the photo albums again. I savored each and every page. It was the beginning of a beautiful trip. I managed to get some sleep that night. Her bed was so comfy. I felt like a very spoiled, rotten kid.

Chapter 35

I have deleted this chapter. I did find out that my birth mom's maternal grandmother was full blood Cherokee. Rejections suck but you know what? It was still very important to find out about my heritage. When my adoptive Mom talked about her (our) Scottish heritage, I never really felt any warmth or excitement. I would never let her know that. I was happy for her. She loved genealogy, but it was not my true heritage.

Chapter 36

Aunt Jeanne and I spent the day with her brother and sister-in-law in Santa Ana. I got to hear a lot more stories. We were going to head to Kalin's in Laguna the next day. After dinner, we sat around that evening and had some laughs. The older clan was ready to go to bed at 9 p.m. I looked at Clayton to see if he wanted to go to Mama Gina's and watch Reno, Larry and band practice for the concert. He said he usually went to bed around nine. It was 9 p.m. and I had no car and no way to get to Mama Gina's. I guess it was bedtime then. Bummer. It was time to read my book.

I was lying in bed at 9:45 pm and if anyone knew me, they would laugh! I have always been a bit of a night owl. I decided to check my phone for some reason and saw that I missed a call from Reno. He said he hoped I would be able to make it tonight. I called back leaving the message that I didn't have a ride over. He called on his break and said, "The whole band kept waiting for you to walk through that door!" Oh wow, what a cool thing to say and how I wished I could have been there. I answered, "Believe me, if I had a car, I would so be there!"

He said that they would probably practice there again tomorrow night. I told him I was going to Kalin's and it would probably be fairly late so I didn't know the chances. I asked if we could meet up early in the day in Corona and he said that would be fine. He said just to give me a call when we get there.

Now it's 10:30 pm and I am going to try and go to sleep! I am tired and had an exhausting day. Back to my book. It's a Dean Koontz book, so excellent story.

Chapter 37

Thursday, July 3, 2008

Today I get to meet my cousins, but more importantly, Kalin! I was so very excited about today. He has been such a wonderful and great brother since he found out about me. He never judged me. He just thought it was cool.

Oh, whoops. I need to back up. Cousin Jay drove up with his wife and 3 beautiful children from San Diego. It was a great afternoon. We sat around the patio and just hung out. We played Bop It! I'm so very bad at it. It was hilarious! Sorry about the jumping around. My mind keeps going a mile a minute.

I looked at Jay and we have the same jaw line. It is so new to me and I just wanted to stare at him. He has more of a prominent chin than I do. He told a story about how someone attached a chin imitating Jay. It was so very funny.

Jay then told a story about how his Grandmother, Signa, gave 3 kisses hello and goodbye because she had 3 sons. We then gave each other 3 kisses goodbye. He's in a band and plays the drums. I told him that I was learning the drums on my own and he told me about DVDs I could rent. I will check it out.

Aunt Jeanne and I left about 4:30 pm to head for Kalin's. This was the pivotal point. He was the one who had been in touch and always accepted me as a sister from the beginning. I was now meeting my brother. I knew we had about a 40- minute drive. I kept trying to wipe the tears from my eyes. This was someone who wanted to get to know me. I had to settle down. I knew I'd be fine. I knew this would be a great evening.

When we arrived, Aunt Jeanne asked if I was ready for this. I just smiled and gave her the thumbs up. Aunt Jeanne and I walked up to the front door and there was my brother with the same big smile as mine. He gave me a hug and a kiss, and I felt so much better. Kalin said, "Wow, I'm so glad that you are here. This is so cool!" All of my anxious, anticipated nerves seemed to settle down, for the most part. We went inside and I met Kalin's fiancé. She was very nice, and I knew that I would be feeling more comfortable as the night progressed.

Then Vallyn and her boyfriend Danny flew in through the front door. Whoa, my sister. I have a son her age. I knew that she didn't know me from anyone, but she came because Kalin asked her to be here. She had her boyfriend with her and he was really nice. Having Aunt Jeanne there helped too.

One of the things I will never forget is Kalin asking me several times during the night, "Are you alright?" He was worried about how I was doing. How was I doing? Quite honestly, I wished I could snap my fingers and make everything freeze so I could catch my breath or wipe a tear or just stare at everyone for a good ten minutes.

Kalin asked me if I wanted a glass of wine. I said, "Well yeah, that would be great." He said he appreciated the fact that I had not brought a bottle of wine to his house. I told him that I knew what he had been through and I would never disrespect him in that way. He joked that he was drinking non-alcoholic beer and he was okay with it. He asked if I wanted some non-alcoholic wine and I said, "Uh, no". He was just kidding. I took my glass of wine and went out to the patio. I met up with Nikki's sister, who was feeling a bit uncomfortable too.

We talked about what was going on in her life. She also talked about how she wanted to come to the islands (San Juan) and work on a project with a friend of hers. I said that she would have the time of her life. I said. "Just feel your heart and see if that is what you want to do." I opened up my home if she came my way.

Kalin was looked at me again and said, "Are you okay?" I kept saying that I was. I felt like I was the little sister

Chapter 38

Bobby Jr. and his wife and two kids arrived. The kids were darling. Luke's the spitting image of me when I was his age. I swear, we could have been twins. I was introduced as a friend of the family's. We went to the backyard and Luke did a little skate boarding. Both Vallyn and her boyfriend showed Luke how to kick up a board. It was very entertaining. When I went back inside, Kalin had presented a rack of lamb with mint jelly along with other appetizers on the dining room table. Wow, he worked so hard. The lamb was perfect and done to perfection. I know he put a lot of effort into this night. There were several other things that he made. And Nikki made wonderful lasagna with quite a bite!

Later when I was outside talking to Nikki's sister Veronica, Kalin came outside and said he had forgotten about the tri tip on the BBQ.

He thought he had cooked it too long. He said, "Oh no I think I cooked it too long!" I said, "It's okay, you and I can take the end pieces, and no one will be the wiser." He said, "I'm doing this all for you!" He was so kind to me.

I did get to visited with Bobby Jr. a bit. He had asked about the concert I was going to on Friday. I had told him Larry Hanson and Reno Bellamy. I said there were "several others like Johnny Lopez, that would be there."

Then I got to share my story with Vallyn. She got to see my non-id papers and all the pics of Bobby and me showing how much we looked alike. I told her that I needed to know my roots and how Kalin and I have been so close for such a long time. She seemed to really accept my story and accept me as a sister. I couldn't have asked for a better night.

I have no idea how Vallyn really felt, but she seemed genuine.

Towards the end of the evening, we took some pictures. I had wished that I had gotten some pics with Bobby Jr. but that's okay. Vallyn was all into taking pics, so we did. I had to make a goofy face but was laughing too hard. Hopefully she got the pic with me being crazy.

It was Aunt Jeanne who told us to grab our cameras. Thankfully we got them out. I got a few very special pictures. I am hoping that Vallyn got some more pictures.

Vallyn said she would keep in touch. It was finally time to leave since everyone else worked the next day. I hugged my brother goodbye. What an incredible effort Kalin put in for this reunion. I don't think he knows how much I appreciated it. I didn't want this night to end but it had to. I walked out with Danny and Vallyn. She said that she knew the story she would keep in touch. She gave me a big hug. I think I just won my sister over, maybe?

Aunt Jeanne and I drove away, and I was in cloud nine. What a wonderful evening! Kalin was everything I thought he would be. What a great brother. And Bobby Jr. and his family were lovely. Kalin put a lot of effort in hoping that I would be accepted by him and his family.

I did stare just a bit. I stared at Vallyn and at Kalin. It was an ominous feeling to see similarities and my heart was feeling so heavy and full. I looked at Kalin's eyebrows, yep, they're mine. Hahaha!

The whole time I thought I had my birth Mom's eyebrows. Then I saw him, dang. I am Hatfield all the way. I can only hope that my sibs grow to accept me. I am my Dad's kid all-the-way.

Tomorrow I go to a concert where a lot of these guys really loved my Father. I am nervous yet excited. I know they will accept me; they already have. This is so crazy meeting people for the first time. It's such a different new connection.

Chapter 39

July 4, 2008

I talked to Reno today and he said that he was going to set up around noon today and we could meet him at any time to pick up the VIP parking pass. Aunt Jeanne and I made it to Santana Park around 12:30 pm...

I saw the guys setting up the stage. I was only 30 feet away. I called Reno on his cell twice and didn't get an answer. Since it was about 104 degrees I decided to go to a shaded tree where Aunt Jeanne could get some shade. We walked about 15 feet and I got a phone call. I turned around and Reno said he thought it was me. He said, "Get over here!"

We walked back over, and Larry and Reno walked down from the stage. I gave Larry a hug and then Reno. Then Larry said, "Could I get another hug?" I said, "Of course!" These guys were feeling the love of Bobby Hatfield. I'm sure it had to be a very happy but sad thing to meet me. I know they were anxious, and they were so very kind. I had such a good feeling.

Reno gave me the VIP parking passes. I told them that Aunt Jeanne and I were going to go to a movie. We said we'd be back around 5 pm. This was going to be another wonderful night!

How I wanted just to stay there and watch them set up. Whoa, I was such a groupie, huh? Aunt Jeanne and I went to a movie and enjoyed the air conditioning on such a hot day. We saw Zohan, pretty funny.

We made it back to the park. We met a lovely girl and she said she was a friend of Reno's. She said to get a sheet laid down and we'd be set. We walked back to the car and grabbed a sheet and a pillow. When we got back, we saw Reno. He introduced us to Bryan and Allen. They both had such big smiles and said it's so nice to finally meet you! They were looking at me like I was something special. It's starting to sink in how many hearts Bobby touched. I realized later that Bryan was one of the lead singers in the band and Allen was the drummer.

We laid out our sheet and got comfortable. We met Reno's wife, sister and granddaughter. The band Southland was playing, and they were great. They are a local southern California band. I have them on MySpace and there are a couple of songs they've written that are incredible.

While I was listening, I saw Reno waving me over. I did the silly, "Me?" gesture and he shook his head yes. Aunt Jeanne said she was comfortable and would wait there. I went backstage and there was Larry. He wanted to see how I was doing. I told him about the funny movie Aunt Jeanne, and I watched and how we loved the air conditioning. He laughed out loud and said, "Yeah, it has been a pretty hot day." We talked for a minute with Reno. He then said he wanted me to meet Barry. I turned around and Barry was sitting in a chair. He stood up, shook my hand and said it was nice to meet me. I said the same and that was about all we talked. Then this gal thumped Reno on the arm and said, "What about me?" Reno then introduced his sister Michaelina to me. She was so funny, ribbing her brother on. What a beautiful lady. I wanted to stay back there longer but didn't want to leave Aunt Jeanne by herself. I popped back out and continued to listen to the music.

I then met DeVonna, Tony (Redbone)'s ex-wife had introduced herself. She's a lovely lady. You could tell she was very close in the family. They all seemed very nice and if I wasn't feeling so timid, I would have mingled more. This was all a bit overwhelming for me. These guys knew and loved my Dad. I didn't get a chance to meet Johnny Lopez but met his wife Sarah who was very down to earth and friendly. I also met a terrific, funny guy named Tom Potts. He grew up with the brothers and was a musician himself. I believe he's pretty good with a camera too!

It was time for Barry Rillera's All Star Band to come on stage. There they were, Johnny Lopez, Larry Hanson, Reno Bellamy, Barry Rillera, Bryan Leicher, Allen Adams and Michaelina Bellamy. I couldn't even tell you the first thing they sang, but I do remember, "Come and Get Your Love", "Sugar Pie Honey Bunch". "Knock on Wood" and some great

Creedance. Wow was I enjoying this. Songs that I knew every word!

Then Michaelina busted out Mustang Sally and more. I wish I had recorded the whole thing. I sure hope someone did. I recorded a little bit with my digital camera. At the end of the show there was a ceremony for a vet and Mikie sang the National Anthem and God Bless America. I was standing next to Reno at the time and he showed me goose bumps on his arm. I assured him I had them all over. She was amazing and I will never forget that.

Reno joked about doing okay up there for a bunch of old guys. I assured him that they were fantastic, and I loved it so much. I got some great pictures. Hopefully they will turn out. Since the sun was shining behind the stage, I took some pictures while they were up on the large monitor. I think those will be good.

While the fireworks were going off, a loud speaker was playing all the famous military songs. It was so inspiring. What a great ending. It was crazy, after six or eight patriotic song, the fireworks were still going.

The fireworks were over, and I could see that Aunt Jeanne was ready to go so I said I just wanted to take a couple of pictures.

Aunt Jeanne didn't know how to use my camera, so I asked a guy named Larry Keister (friend of Reno's) to take the pictures. Reno and I got a pic first and didn't know it but Mikie jumped in the picture. She was sneaky. She totally cracked me up! There she was, ha, ha, ha! Then Larry Hanson walked up and we spoke a moment and then I said picture time. He said he was kind of sweaty from packing the stuff, but I said it didn't matter. Then we got a pic of Larry, Mikie, Reno and me.

Reno then introduced me to Larry Keister as Bobby Hatfield's daughter. I looked at him and he was so excited to meet me. It was like I was this movie star that everyone loved. But believe me, I take no credit. I was just lucky enough to look like Bobby Hatfield. I won't forget this day as long as I live. I wish my family could have experienced it too. That was the first time I was introduced as Bobby Hatfield's daughter.

It was then time to say my goodbyes and head back with Aunt Jeanne. I gave Reno and Larry a hug goodbye. Reno said this was only the beginning. I said that I would keep in touch and thanked them again for everything. I so didn't want to walk away but it was time. But really, will I ever be in the same city as Larry and Reno again? Who knows, maybe they'll all come to Seattle. Hey, it could happen!

When Aunt Jeanne and I got home she was pretty beat as she should be. She did mention how Clayton was watching my hands the other night and they reminded him so much of his Uncle Bob. I thought that was very interesting since I have watched his videos and have seen a lot of ways, he would move his hands like mine. There goes those genetics again. She said good night and I helped myself to a glass of wine and crawled into bed. I looked at the pictures over and over and re-lived the night. Wow, I had such a great day!

Tomorrow I would be going home. This trip went by so fast, but I am anxious to get back to my family. I have missed them and wished they could have experienced, what I had.

Chapter 40

Saturday July 5, 2008

Since Aunt Jeanne had a hair appointment in Palm Springs we have decided to see if I could get an earlier flight. The plan was to drop me off with some friends of hers (actually best friends) and they would take me to the airport. It worked out fine. I said my goodbyes to my favorite Aunt and met her best friends. They were lovely people. They wanted to hear my story so over coffee and a great blueberry muffin, I pulled out my book. I explained everything and they were enthralled. They said that they knew my Father and I was very much like him. I felt good about that.

So off we went to the airport. They helped me with my bags and then I went up to the outside counter to see if I could get an earlier flight. I looked back and they were just staring at me with concerned eyes. How sweet is that? Aunt Jeanne put them in charge of me. I told them that I was okay and that I would be fine. I promised. I told them to go ahead and leave and after the third time, they did. I felt like a kid. It was very sweet.

They got me into a 12-noon flight, it's now 11:30 am. The guy said he was supposed to charge me but would be a nice guy. Maybe it was my smile. I blessed him, ha!

I got to my gate and found out the flight is delayed one half hour. Who cares, I'll be home earlier than I thought! I called Pete and told him the scoop. He was thrilled that I'll be home earlier than planned. We finally boarded the plane and took off. I just left the people I just met and that I love. I was equally anxious to get home to my family and tell them about my trip. Even though I spoke to my husband each day, there was more for me to fill in. I was going to continue to get to know my new-found family. I was not sad that I was leaving, I was sad that I didn't know the next time I will see them again.

Part Five

Home Sweet Home

Chapter 41

I made it home and got hugs and kisses from my whole family including my g babe...I missed him so. My two beautiful sons, my gorgeous daughter and fabulous husband were so welcoming. Home, sweet home. We had a BBQ and firework party to get ready for. My friends, Frank and Debra, along with their parents were coming up. We had a few other friends coming up too. The kids didn't want to do fireworks without me, so they held off until tonight. Yay!

What a show they put on! Wow, I loved every minute of it. We sat around the bonfire and felt the warmth of the fire. We had to scoot back each time they threw a new pallet on. Once in a while Nick threw some firecrackers in the fire and scared the living daylights out of us!

And then after the show we did some karaoke. Everyone was singing at the top of their lungs and we all sounded fantastic! Funny how much better we sounded after a few libations.

All in all, it was a great time, and everyone loved it. We kept the bonfire going till the wee hours. Home sweet home.

Chapter 42

I mentioned the MySpace page of The Righteous Brothers and the gal managing it was Katy. She has kept my secret and we have been in touch quite a bit. I will know when the time is right, when I share my adoption journey. I will probably not publish this until after my parents have passed.

Back to Katy, we hit it off beautifully and said she would have Jimmy contact me when she talks to him next.

The point of me talking about her was that we were both realizing how different things are at our ends of the world. Little things that I took for granted like, bodysurfing, tri-tip roasts, Eggs Benedict, Mimosas…she had no clue what they were. I still laugh when I think about telling her about Father's Day. I told her we had Mimosas and Eggs Benedict. She emailed back and said she and Chris didn't know what Eggs Benedict was but aren't Mimosas boiled egg with mayonnaise? Ha, ha, ha, so funny!

It has been a real education and a lot of fun communicating with her. It has also been a delight. I hope to meet her someday. She sent a picture of Chris and Jimmy Page the other day. My fifteen- year-old son Nick was very thrilled about it. The Yardbirds were doing a concert and Jimmy showed up. So that was cool. Pete and Nick went to the concert. I had to work.

By the way, I told her to Wikipedia tri-tip and she did. She went to the butcher and he still couldn't figure it out after she showed the guy a picture of a steer and all its parts. I also had her look up bodysurfing on you tube and she was blown away.

To me, it's something I grew up doing. I thought everyone knew about it. I know I will continue to be in contact with her hopefully for many years to come. I think she's actually some kind of reporter because she interviewed Jimmy Walker years back and they hit it off. Right now, I have trusted her with my story.

Chapter 43

July 25, 2008

I have had so many things going through my brain. I presume I am a typical adoptee. When I got home from my trip to California, Vallyn had accepted me as a friend on MySpace. I was thrilled. I decided to email her and leave a brief message. She was in Kauai at the time but that was okay. I reiterated that I was so glad that I was able to explain my story and how everything came about. I explained that I thought long and hard about how she could be feeling. She was the only daughter as long as she has lived, then in comes... me. I told her that I understood any hesitations she would have. I was sorry that her mother was ill, and we weren't able to meet. I said that if Linda wanted to contact me by email or phone that I would be very happy to speak with her.

Well, that was around July 6th or so. I have not heard back from her yet. Now I must remember that she is a 26-year-old girl that has a lot going on, but this is where paranoia sets in as an adoptee. I am so grateful that I have a wonderful, loving family or this would drive me crazy. Right now, it just sits at the back of my head. I haven't heard back from Kalin for a few days, but that was typical. We usually kept in touch about once a week. We both got busy and sometimes a bit of time passed before we caught up.

I received a lovely message from Aunt Jeanne. She said she loved every minute that I was down there and missed and loved me. She said Clayton received the pictures I sent. Then mentioned the general consensus was that Kalin and I looked most alike. Of course, I loved that. He had my heart. Aunt Jeanne was up at her sister's in San Francisco. I haven't called her back due to my hectic time at work, but hopefully I will get through to her tomorrow. I needed to let her know how much I missed her and loved her too. What an incredible lady! Everyone should have an Aunt Jeanne. One of God's great gifts on earth. Thank you, thank you God.

I must have got some great photos at the Barry Rillera's All Star Band concert. I posted a bunch of pics. A few days later I looked on Reno's MySpace to see if he had more pics. I was looking and thinking, "Wow, that looked like the pic I took. Hey that looked just like my pic. Okay I took that same pic on the monitor." He must have liked them because he took all my pics and put them on his website. I was very happy that he loved my pics.

I decided to look at his pics (mine) and there was a pic of Larry Hanson and Bobby Hatfield's daughter Sheri for the entire world to see! I just sat at my computer and cried my eyes out...again. There I was. Acknowledgment, I was Bobby Hatfield's daughter. I can't really explain how I felt. I guess honored, proud, loved and overwhelmed at the same time. I apologize if I have used overwhelmed too many times, but I don't think I could describe it any differently. It's a good thing. It's not like being overwhelmed at work. The overwhelming feeling that I have been getting was love and respect from my new family.

I have a friend who is always asking for updates on my life. He always says to me, "How's Sheri-land?" That cracks me up. I had to respond that Sheri-land was doing just fine and my little world was rockin'.

I had to work through Monday and then Tuesday morning, Pete, Nick and I take off for Kauai. Wow, it came up so fast. I haven't really thought about it and now it's here. I loved the idea that I didn't have to worry about my crew of 42 and their issues. And I meant that in the most loving way. I'm very happy being Dear Abby and a great shoulder to lean on, but at least once a year, I need to let go.

I have known some young men who never got a hug as they grew up. No show of loving emotion. Well, I am so very huggy. When I found that out I told two brothers, "Guess what? You are going to get a hug a day from me from now on!" Every day, they come to me for that hug. Affection is so very important, and I have watched these two boys blossom. I love these kids. There may be other employees that think we're a bit weird for being affectionate, but they probably just needed a hug.

Reno sent me a great picture of him playing the congas in an Elton John Tribute. He looked like the bomb, Joe Cool himself. I guess they had an after party with all five siblings there at a restaurant doing karaoke etc. Tony (T-Bone) Bellamy of Redbone sang, "Come and Get Your Love" which got the crowd crazy. So very cool, good for them. One of Reno's brothers was a DJ in Vegas so that worked out well. I was so happy that the gig went well and that all was good.

Reno ended it with LOL SIS. Okay I liked that. To be called sis and I knew he meant it, was very cool. It pounded on my heart a bit. It looked like Reno was very close to his four siblings and that's a blessing.

I was heading to Kauai with my husband and 15-year - old son Nick. We would be gone to two weeks and doing a lot of hiking, snorkeling, swimming and surfing (if my son has his way). Just one more day of work.

I'm not going to think about anything except for the sand, surf and sea.

God bless vacations...

Chapter 44

July 28, 2008

Well, I did it. I got through the last day of the work week. Tomorrow morning at 5:30 am, I will be getting ready to leave for Kauai. My oldest son Brandon is driving us down. I wish he and Sarah were going too. Of course, that would include a free flight for little Evan who just turned one.

I don't know if I have shared this story before but again MySpace has introduced me to so many new friends. I don't really even remember how I met Richard Filaccio. He is a singer/songwriter. Somehow, I ran across him. I asked him today how we met, and he was going to check back in his notes.

He wrote a song years ago called, "There Goes Pete Best". Peter and the Penguins from Norway sing a beautiful version of it. The Penguins sound very Beatle-ish, great band. Richard started The Pop League on my space for a lot of talented unsigned artists which include the Penguins.

Ironically, I found out that Pete Best was coming to our casino for a concert. I let Richard know and he couldn't believe it! He wrote the song so many years ago and wished somehow that he could get a copy to him and explain the lyrics. I said I would be happy to try and give Pete the CD after his concert. Richard was so excited! He wrote a nice letter and sent it with the CD to me about a week before the concert. I was very nervous about delivering the CD to Pete Best, but it was a great song!

The night of the concert arrived. The band was great! Pete was on the drums and the lead singers were great. There was a lot of talent in the room. After the concert, my mouth was a bit dry and I was very nervous. I had my friend and co-worker go with me to meet him. I got a picture with him and had him sign the book I had bought, his biography. Once he finished, I handed him the CD and said that a friend of mine wrote a song about him. He thanked me, and we were out of there.

So that was that. I emailed Richard the chain of events, but I made it happen. Would he listen to it that night and love it? Would he be insulted and take it as a jab? It was just an unfortunate chain of events for him. Richard asked 1000 questions and I tried to give him all the detail I could. I sent him the pictures we took and then sent him the book that Pete signed. Richard deserved the book much more than me. He was thrilled.

Life was in limbo for the next week, not knowing if he liked it or not. Then Richard got a call from Pete Best's manager saying that she was going to sue him if he didn't take the song off my space. She said it was slander and it was a defamation of character. She continued to say that they would sue him if he and the Penguins didn't take everything off of their websites.

Richard panicked and emailed me to tell me what went on. He said that he removed the song and so did Peter and the Penguins. I felt so bad for Richard as well as the Penguins. I'm thinking, "Hey, you did nothing wrong. You just told a story." One of the things that offended Pete was that Pete was hanging out in a seedy bar called "The Losers Club". I am no one to judge. I know I would feel bad if someone wrote a demeaning song about me. But he was definitely unlucky.

A couple of weeks later Richard says "Screw it. It was just a phone call. I didn't get served with anything. It was just a threat over the phone. There Goes Pete Best is going back on MySpace." I was thrilled to hear that.

It was too good of song to go by the wayside.

A few weeks later Peter and the Penguins went to the Cavern in Liverpool and performed that great song. The response was huge and I am just waiting for them to load it on YouTube. Peter and the Penguins are hoping to get their CD done this year and then it will become world renown. Such wonderful people I have met on this journey of mine. That reminds me, I needed to look up that song on YouTube.

Chapter 45

August 17, 2008

Kauai was an amazing trip. Every day we went to someplace new. We would end up at one of our favorite places by the end of the day. Kauai is the only island with loads of rivers. What an unbelievable sight to see a river run right to the ocean. We used each day for new discoveries. Between the waterfalls, beaches and lush surroundings, it was so hard to leave. We got tons of snorkeling in too. Pete and I have a trick to make fish gather around.

Last Thursday I got back to work feeling rested, tan and sassy. I was ready to get back in the swing of things. Later that week I got a call from my old Director who went to work at a casino close to my home. He basically offered me the Guest Services Manager job, but I had to go through the hoops. So, after six and a half years, I was moving on. I would only be 15 minutes away instead of 45, yay!

What does this have to do with my adoption? Absolutely nothing, but it is the way my life evolved since my birth Mom gave me up for adoption. I don't know where I would have been if my mother kept me.

Oh yeah, I talked with my Aunt Jeanne the other day. She said how much she loved me and missed me staying at her condo. Boy so do I. We had so much fun. I sent her pics and she loved them. She was going to catch up with Kalin and Vallyn. She asked if Kalin and I were keeping in touch. I said like clockwork. I told her I hadn't heard from Vallyn but knew that she had just come back from Kauai too. Vallyn and I seemed to really have hit it off but she could have changed her mind about wanting to get to know me more. Who knows? I invaded her life as the only daughter of Bobby Hatfield. I did email her after I got home and told her that I really enjoyed our time together and was glad that I was able to explain how I found out about myself. She seemed to really accept it all. She has a MySpace so I may have to send her a note.

It is a blessing for me because I have longed all my life to look like someone. I have heard more and more lately that my daughter and I look alike and of course I love that. She's drop dead gorgeous! There are very strong resemblances of the Strobaugh side, but I think some of the Hatfield side has come through.

Chapter 46

August 23, 2008

We had some exciting news today. A couple of months ago my husband emailed a girl with the last name Strobaugh and asked if by chance we could be related. She just answered today. Come to find out, Pete has a ½ brother that he never knew about! He knows he has a ½ sister named Tina but had no idea about his brother John Franklin Strobaugh.

The story is just unfolding but according to his daughter, he never knew he had any siblings at all. It was always just Dad and the girls as Strobaughs. So now we have been introduced, through MySpace, he has A LOT more family. Angel is John's daughter. We found out he goes by Jeff. She is going to let her Dad know the news and hopefully he'll be calling Pete sometime soon. The more family the better and I'm not quite sure how many times I have said that.

Chapter 47

September 7, 2008

There is a new show called, "The Locater". I wonder how many adoptees and birthparents have watched with uncomfortable anticipation. So many thoughts have been going through my head and I haven't even watched it.

On occasion, I email through MySpace a musician or song writer hoping they might have a special story about my Dad. I wrote one singer/songwriter who will remain nameless. I told him who I was and asked if he knew my Father. Here was his response: Hi Sheri, A huge, huge apology for not writing sooner. I've never really looked at the mail on my MySpace account…it was started for me and I never got in the habit… I just logged on and found a mountain of messages. I wanted to answer yours right away.

I loved your Dad. He and Willy (I don't know why I've always called Bill Willy) were one of the first brilliant teams I ever heard. I can close my eyes and see them coming onstage from opposite wings...singing, "There's a rockin' little monkey name of Koko Joe...or "Talking about my baby not your baby..." They were amazing and Bobby's voice was angelic.

We had way too much fun!!!! All of us. I saw your Dad in Vegas a few weeks before he died. It was a shock and a terrible loss. He was one of the really good guys. I'm still close to the Medleys... I play in Vegas now and then for Michael G. and your Dad and Bill are probably responsible for that.

My personal email is ***********@aol.com. I hope you are well and that you'll forgive my late, late, late response. I send blessings to you and yours."

What a lovely letter to get from him. I really was thrilled to receive such kind and loving words. Now this guy would have some wonderful stories to share. I wondered if he would consider getting together sometime and tell me about my Dad. I went ahead and emailed him back through his personal email and thanked him so much for responding to me.

I explained how I found out about my birth Father and how I was getting to know the family. I said how wonderful it was to learn new things about my Father. I said that Bill had been very kind to me and hoped he would share more with me in the future. I told him that I would love to come out and see one of his shows in Vegas in the near future.

I NEVER heard back from him. How lame was that. He found out that I was a love child and it ended right there. He could have given Bill Medley a phone call. What is wrong with people? Did he think I was an extortionist or something? If my Dad was alive, I would probably not have the same adverse effect on people. This is one of the reasons why adoption makes our lives awkward, uncomfortable, insecure. I have heard so many stories where adoptees feel that they just don't fit. They don't fit with their adopted families and they don't fit with their birth families. I have been very blessed to have given birth to four lovely children and have been married to the same wonderful man for many years. That is enough for me.

There are good people out there and one of them is Pete Townsend. The Who was rumored to be touring soon and they are my son Nick's all-time favorite and of course mine. He can play every song on his guitar and he's very good. We got him a replica of Pete's guitar.

I decided to send Pete Townsend a fan letter. I asked if there was any way to get my son a backstage pass to see them. I said that he got the same electric guitar as him and played The Who music every day. Then I did it, I name dropped! I told him my son was Bobby Hatfield's grandson and inherited some great talent. I thought, why not finally do a name drop.

I wrote with red ink and put the fan letter in a red envelope, hoping that would catch his attention.

Apparently, it did! I heard back from the great legend, Pete Townsend. He sent an autographed picture for my son and wrote me a note that said, "Your Dad and I crossed paths in England years back on a television show. He was a lovely man."

That was very cool and wonderful surprise. My son was thrilled too! No mention of a back-stage pass, but I honestly didn't think I would get a response in the first place. Thank you, Pete Townsend! You are a kind gentleman.

Chapter 48

September 10, 2008

Yahoo! I got the job! I'm so very excited about the whole thing. I was told that people are really excited about me starting and that they heard about me. What a good feeling.

My new boss actually called my old boss to let them know they offered me the job. My new boss told me that he never met anyone better at customer service than me. What a compliment! We used to work together. So, in turn he probably told the GM. It still will be incredibly uncomfortable at work tomorrow. They will either accept my two-week's notice or escort me out. It made my stomach turn...

My family is so excited!! We celebrated with a great pasta dinner! I cooked a six-hour marinara. I emailed my brother Kalin about my new adventure and he was so stoked! His email was wonderful. I will let them know too. I will call my Mom and Dad tomorrow too. They always worried about me commuting so far. My commute now will be only be ten-fifteen minutes! I have had to drive through snowstorms over the last six years. Now Pete can drive me when it snows, yay!

I just have to get through tomorrow to see how the next two weeks are going to take place. I filled out my application for my Class II license and it says to state my parent's names then also step-parent names. My husband says, "What about birth parent's names?" He was half joking but it was an odd feeling. I had thought about it too.

Now getting back to "The Locater". Wow, what a tough thing to watch for any adoptee or birthparent. I did make sure I was alone. Well, I was not alone, but Pete was definitely sound asleep.

I didn't just watch once, but twice at two different times. I had the same reaction both times. Luckily this time, the birthmother was so very grateful to be able to see her daughter again. The birth daughter met her sisters and father, and it was emotionally draining but such a blessing.

This was a show that I will record and watched every episode. I felt tortured but at the same time I will be so very happy for each adopted one with a happy ending. I am blessed with a happy ending because I had my brother, Kalin, and my Aunt Jeanne. I do have family on my Mom's side that I won't get to know, but I am grateful for what God has given me.

I will say goodbye for now since tomorrow is going to be a very interesting day.

Chapter 49

September 11, 2008

It's hard to believe that so many years have passed since 9-11. It is all so very sad and so many people died. I believe the total came to about 2700. I could be wrong. I thought about all of the families and their losses. It gave me a stomachache to watch the news this morning where they showed the planes hitting the towers. It was such a horrific tragedy. Also, to remember Pennsylvania and the Pentagon, this didn't get mentioned as much. When I start to feel sorry about this or that, I have to remember how blessed I have been. I have a beautiful family and my health.

I made it through my day and gave official notice. My boss came into the office and gave me a hug. And trust me on this, he was not a huggy person. I have probably gotten 4 hugs in the 10 years I've known him. He wished the best for me and said his resume was out there and we had to look out for what's best for ourselves.

I had to go find the Asst. GM. I've known him for over 10 years, and I know he really doesn't want me to go. I went to Human Resources and found him and a few HR gals. He just looked at me. I said, "I love you", and hugged him. He turned to the ladies and said I gave notice. One gal (his wife) hugged me and said she was thrilled that I got the job! The other two had sad faces. So, what do I do? I start crying. And that is when I said, "Okay, I've got to go!" Andy (Asst. GM) says, "I need to talk to you". I agreed.

Andy has always been an absolutely wonderful man. I worked for him the first time 11 years ago and he promoted me and understood my potential for guest services. I was on a special task force with all of the Directors to come up with new innovative ways to enhance our guests' experiences. Andy also used to work for Harrah's back in the day when The Righteous Brothers were performing. He would go in the showroom after his shift and hear them play. Then he would sit back and visit with them. He said he had many nights just shooting the breeze. He told me that my father was a wonderful guy with a great voice. Andy has been married to a beautiful woman named Cindy who works in the HR office. I will surely miss my Silver Reef family. An added note, my father is the smartest man I have ever known. Andy takes second place.

It was a small world. Someone that I have been very close to, actually hung out with my birth dad several times, weird. I asked him one time who was his favorite and he said, "The Righteous Brothers!" He had a huge smile on his face, and I knew he was just thinking back in time. He said he would dig back in his closet and find The Righteous Brothers albums and give them to me. That's cool. Little does he know that I have bought (through Ebay) almost every album The Righteous Brothers made!

I have another friend that wanted me to list every album that I have because he is hoping to find one that I don't have. I just love the effort and the friendship. I needed to make a list for him. I have been promising that for about three months. I will do it, I promise Lloyd!

I know that there are so many feelings that I never thought I would feel. So many things that I promised myself I wouldn't let bug me. So many insecurities and I know I shouldn't have. It was too much over thinking.

September 12, 2008

I have had an emotional day. The word had spread like wildfire that I am leaving. A lot of tears were shed today. I have three slot attendants that want to follow me. But they can't, it's too far and I have told them that I will stay in touch and continue to send them hugs.

One piece of music that has always be relaxing to me is Larry Hanson's "Canyon Hotel". For some reason, it put me at ease. It's brilliant. I hope it gets out there. Check it out on his MySpace page.

That led me to a thought. I know that Bobby Hatfield's my birth Dad and its crazy how much we look alike. I don't know how many people believe that there has been a reason for everything and a plan. Why have so many things happened to me since I found out who I was? I was meant to find my siblings. I was meant to finally see a man that looked so much like me. I was meant to meet his wonderful life-long friends like Reno Bellamy, Larry Hanson, Bill Medley and many others.

What an extraordinary time in my life and I do know the reason I have had such confidence wasn't out of vanity or me being full of myself. It was from being comfortable with who I was. Finding out that I have a legend for a birth Father does put a little hop in my step though, even though few knew about me. Heehee.

Chapter 50

October 5, 2008

I haven't written for a few weeks but that doesn't mean it's been boring. Actually, it's been quite the opposite.

My husband, Pete, lost touch with his very best friend about 18 years ago. He had moved and we couldn't find him. Somehow, he found our number and called Pete the other day. They talked non-stop for about an hour. It was like they had never been apart. I hadn't seen Pete that happy for a long time.

Aaron still lives in Florida and will be picking Pete up from the airport. What a wonderful trip he'll have. I wish I could share it with him but I just started a new job and there's no way I could get the time off.

My oldest son Brandon originally had plans to go to Orlando to meet a friend there. He has made arrangements, so he'll be able to make it to the wedding also with Pete and Nick. I'm so glad he's going. He deserves a little bit of fun.

Pete gets to see his very best friend, a brother he never knew existed, meet his new nieces and go to his nephew's wedding that he's known since he was born. Sounds like a wonderful trip to me! And they get to go scalloping!

As for me, I am on a new adventure! I was given a wonderful going away party with cake and presents from my dear friends at work. It was a very tearful event, but I made it through. Six and a half years is a long time and I have built very strong bonds with so many.

Last week, I started at the new casino. My new boss has been wonderful. He had my cell phone and computer all set up when I got there. He took me to lunch, and I didn't feel like I got anything done the first day. The rest of the week I wrote job descriptions for my new department. On Friday, my boss said Happy Friday to me. I said, "Oh no, it's just my Thursday. I'll be back tomorrow." He said, "Sheri, you kicked ass this week. Take tomorrow off." Wow, I wasn't going to say no to that.

The only disappointment I have had was that I was really hoping to go to G2E, the biggest national gaming show held in Las Vegas each year.

I had ulterior motives. Reno Bellamy and Bertie Higgins were playing at the Texas Station Casino on the weekends. I really wanted to go see their show. I told Reno that I would probably be there in November, but now I'll have to figure something else out. Reservations had already been made and I was the new kid on the block, so I guess it wouldn't look right. He did promise to take me next year, so that's cool.

I watched, "The Locator" again after everyone was in bed. It's good that I do that because I haven't been dried eyed yet. It really was enlightening too because not all of the reunions are perfect. One was about a Father who was basically a flake. He said that it was up to his daughter to reunite with him and when she was ready, then that was fine. He got put into his place by the locator as he should have. It makes me think of my family.

Every time I look into my children's eyes, I love them even more. Brandon is very intense, athletic and loves the adrenalin rush. Sarah is a wonderful mother of two and is the Manager of a Starbucks. She's the typical middle child, very grounded. Nick is my artistic one who plays the electric guitar and loves playing Xbox and has picked up Bobby's musical talents. All three are very different. I have loved watching them grow.

I know I will continue with this adventure and many more wonderful things will come my way.

I think I have come a long way since I found out who my birth parents were. I have felt the exact same way as I did for my parents prior to my discovery. No surprise there. They raised me, nurtured me and loved me unconditionally. We have always been very close, and I wish I could tell them. But what good would it do? It would cause undue stress and worry. They worry about every little thing and that would just be selfish.

I was hoping to have (like every other adoptee) the perfect fairytale ending when finding my birth family. I wanted them to all fly up and be as anxious as I was to meet them. It took me time to realize I just interrupted their lives with a huge shock. Who was this lady claiming to be Bobby Hatfield's daughter?

I am incredibly sad that I never got to meet my birth father but very lucky to have endless videos and pictures of him. I never knew how I was going to feel when watching him on TV. I would see him rub his thumb with his forefinger the way I have always done, or wiggle the way I have always wiggled, or smile with my same smile, or move the way I have always done. Most of the time though, watching him made me smile.

What I do know is that I have my family, my husband, children, parents, grandbaby and friends. And I am blessed with my new family.

I have new friends who deeply loved my birth father. They will fill in the gaps as I need them filled. They have sent me stories as I needed to hear them. They have been wonderful angels who have entered my life. For this, I am truly blessed and incredibly lucky. I know that they are friends for a lifetime.

I made the decision to search. Not because I didn't have a wonderful childhood growing up. Not because I don't love my parents and brothers dearly. Not because I wanted to find something better.

I made the decision to search because I needed to know where I came from. I needed to know where my ancestors were from. I needed to know how my family health history was. I needed to know if I had to be concerned about anything. I needed to know if anyone looked like ME...

What I didn't know was that I would get an un-relenting need to find my birth family after reading my non-identification information from the Children's Home Society of California. I didn't sleep for the first few nights after reading my information over and over. I didn't know that it would spiral into a search that I needed to do. And I didn't know that after just one week, I would be staring at my birth name.

I have one more battle to deal with. I have decided that I want a copy of my original birth certificate.

I received a call back from the Children's Home Society last week. I had asked what form I needed to get to receive my original birth certificate. She said that my birth records were a ward of the state. I would have to appeal to the Superior Court to have them released. There would have to be a good reason that I needed the original documents to be released.

A good reason for "my" birth records to be released? Let me think a minute, oh yeah, it is my right to have my own birth records. Now I see why there are so many groups advocating open records. I didn't want to do this, but I did find out that I am 1/8 Cherokee. I have heard that I can get my birth records released because of my native blood. I guess that will be my next challenge. A new adventure. Life is a challenge, and I am ready for the next one.

Chapter 51

October 8, 2008

I was looking back through my emails trying to figure out when Kalin's birthday was. I knew it was the middle of the month but not sure of the date. I couldn't find it but what I did find out was exactly two years ago today I found out that my birth name was Pamela Lee Hatfield. Happy birthday to me! I will remember that date now for the rest of my life. These last two years have gone by fast but not without a huge range of emotions, mostly good.

I want to tell everyone at work about my new birthday, but only one person there knows about my birth father. I want to keep it special and share only with those I feel comfortable. I've only been there for 2 weeks so it's not like they're family yet. That's okay. Happy Birthday to me!

October 14, 2008

I wrote Vallyn on MySpace about two weeks ago. I saw that she didn't get on the site too often, but I wanted to try again to communicate with her. We got along so beautifully on the day we met. It felt comfortable and good.

I heard from her today! It was great! She quit her other job three months prior. That is where I originally wrote her. She wrote me a nice long letter and I am just thrilled that she wants to get to know me.

She asked me if I knew about the star that The Righteous Brothers were being honored with in front of Disneyland. I said yes. Kalin had sent me an article about it and Clayton said that he and Aunt Jeanne were planning on going also. It's the Anaheim Walk of Stars. Local celebrities and The Righteous Brothers were the 9th to be honored with a star.

Kalin said he would try to get a video and send it to me. That would be cool. It would be even cooler if I hopped a plane and flew down there but that was not a possibility. I'm not quite sure how my reception would be received either. I'm still a secret to the public and was not invited. But it's not like I had to tell anyone. I could have just been a friend of the family. I was the birth daughter of Bobby Hatfield, so again I have felt, awkward, insecure and stuck in the middle of nowhere.

I turned myself around and instead of jumping on the pitiful me train, I decided to make my parents' favorite meal. They live an hour away, so we go up every other weekend and bring lunch. Dad especially likes my Chile Verde Chicken Enchiladas so that was what they got. Topped with sour cream and fresh avocados. I felt wonderful and Pete and I were glad to spend the day with them.

October 15, 2008

Today, The Righteous Brothers received their star. Still feeling bummed that I wasn't invited to watch the honor live, I kept trying to shake it off. They've only known about me for a couple of years. Maybe it was just too much of a public place for me to be at this time. I would have kept it on the down low. Oh well.

I haven't heard how it went yet, but I know the family had to be proud. It will be so special to see next time I'm down there. It kind of makes my stomach hurt when I think about it though. I don't know why. I know that I will be visiting his grave when I'm down there next. Of course, that will be hard, but the good things are hard too. Just reminds me more and more how I never met him. I know he is sending me kisses from heaven. I just wish I could feel them.

I plan to keep writing down my journey. I hope that I have helped, in some way, other adoptees and birth parents understand all of the emotions, insecurities, joys, fears and overwhelming feelings that come and go on a whim. I have always been such a strong person and have been completely knocked for a loop over the times I have melted in a Moment over some comment or a picture or a thought.

Part six

Update

Chapter 52

August 2011

It had now been five years since I found out I was the birth daughter of Bobby Hatfield. I received a wonderful email from Kalin. The Clem Colonists at Anaheim Union High School were honoring Robert (Bobby) Hatfield. Wow, how exciting! What a wonderful thing and so deserving. Kalin said he and the siblings were going. He wanted to know if Pete and I could make it down. What? I was invited! Yes! I would most certainly make it happen. Pete told me to go ahead and go. He was too busy at the time and said he'd hold down the fort.

I couldn't breathe. I was invited by the family to go to a gathering honoring my dad! There would be all of his old friends there. I could see a lot of old pics. There would probably be tons of memorabilia there. This was the moment I was waiting for, to be accepted as one of the Hatfield kids. This was going to be a day for the books.

Kalin said that Aunt Jeanne was going along with her two sons and daughter in law. I asked my girlfriend to go with me too. No problem there. She said she would be honored. She lived in Palm Spring also, so I planned on flying into that airport.

I put in for the time off and got okayed right away. This was going to be very cool, especially since I was included in the celebration. They have no idea how good it feels to be included!

I received an email back from Janet, who was in charge of the event. I had asked her to make sure we were at Kalin's table per his request. She said, "Just to make sure, you are one of Bobby's children?" I told her that I was but even though the world didn't know about me, my siblings did. She thanked me for the information.

I flew down a couple of days early and stayed with Gina. The weather was warm and perfect. We met up with Kalin in the parking lot and he immediately held my hand. We walked through the parking lot together. We reached the reception table and then were led to our table up front. Kalin said we were sitting with him. Again, I felt like the little sister. He made me more comfortable and I thank him for that.

The room had tons of memorabilia. They did a great job in decorating. A lot of high school pictures of Bobby were scattered around. Very fun. You could tell that Bobby's Class of 1958 was very proud of him!

Dinner was served and was delicious. I looked around and there were a lot of eyeballs looking at me. Okay. Fine with me. Maybe they thought I was a cousin or something. While eating, a gentleman at our table asked who I was. I told him I was Bobby's daughter. He seemed very confused. I felt too bad for him. I realized that he had 5 x 7 cards in his hands and was probably the speaker. Poor guy, what was he thinking right now? Do I add her to my speech? Do I change anything? It was all good. He just did his speech as usual and my name didn't come up. But, ha, ha, ha, every time I took a bite, I felt his eyeballs on me.

At the end of the speech, he asked the family to come up. Kalin grabbed me by the arm and said, "You are coming up here with us. Aunt Jeanne said, "Let's go!" We were all up there, Kalin, Dustin, Vallyn, Aunt Jeanne, Jay, Gina and...me.

Vallyn was given the microphone and thank everyone for the honor. She said, "On behalf of my brothers and myself, we thank you." It was all good that she didn't include me. The world didn't know about me.

Cocktails were served and a lot of mingling went on after that. I was approached by several people. They said they knew about me. They said that both my parents were really lovely people. They were so pleased to meet me. I told them and I was just honored to be part of this celebration. A couple of Bobby's friends shared a story about sports or choir. They ended up with tears in their eyes as they got choked up. Of course, that got me choked up. What a blessed evening to have with many of Bobby's old classmates.

I knew that there were more people out there that knew about me. How could there not be? That just proved it. I appreciated how kind they were about it. I had a lot of people who kept staring at me that night, but most came up and spoke to me. One of the gals pointed out a past high school buddy. She said, "If you ever want any gossip about anything, just ask Sheila (named changed)." Hahahaha! That was so funny. I was tempted to speak with her, just for a story or two. Now, I wish I had.

It was a great night. I met so many people that night and a lot of them just wanted to rub my arm and give me a smile. It was very humbling. I would chalk that up to one of my favorite nights.

I managed to get together with Aunt Jeanne for lunch before I flew back. We laughed about what people were probably thinking. She noticed that people were staring at me and whispering. I just hope it livened up their lives a bit and added some excitement in their elderly days.

I had an easy flight back. I sat there in solitude and thought about my trip. I remembered the loving and gentle things Aunt Jeanne said to me. I remembered Kalin sliding his hand into mine in the parking lot, before we entered the Anaheim HS Reunion, honoring our Dad. He knew I was nervous. I remembered wiping a tear from an old classmate of

Bobby's after he shared a tender Moment. I remembered giving that gentleman a kiss on the cheek.

A couple of days after I flew back, I received some pictures that Steve Valdez had taken. He was a very nice guy and so helpful when I was planning the trip down. Thank you, Steve.

Chapter 53

I was forwarded an email about one of the guys that knew Bobby very well in high school and he was going to be the speaker and inductor. I thought I would add this.

Hi Geri,

I don't know if you have talked to Janet recently, but she called me. She was searching for someone to induct Bobby. I gave her a few names to contact including Gary D. Gary knows a lot about Bob. As I remember the two of them used to harmonize well at Curry's Ice Cream Shop across from Fremont and the fast food place (still there) on the corner of Citron and Center, just across the street from the school. I also gave her Marilyn P's phone number. She mentioned that several of Bob's relatives would be in attendance.

Bobby always demonstrated an aptitude and interest in entertaining. He was at ease in front of groups -in the classroom, in the school assemblies, in musical performances and on the field of play. We all enjoyed his sense of humor. His social skills and popularity made him a shoe in for being selected as our Student Body President. At Anaheim H.S. Bobby played football, basketball and baseball. While he was a good player in all three sports, he excelled in baseball. If he hadn't found his musical niche, he very well may have ended up in professional baseball.

How did he develop his athletic skills? Anaheim in those years had wonderful after school and summer city park programs. There was a group of us that played sports from the age of 5-6 until we graduated from H.S. The City Park (now Pearson Park) was the place to meet nearly every day in the summer months. In those days, we would leave home in the morning and arrive back home for dinner.

When our group of boys reached about age 13 years, La Palma Park became our meeting place. It was at La Palma where we were able to play a morning baseball game five days per week during the summer months. Bobby was one of the players who played on Anaheim's Midget and Junior All-Star baseball teams and later on the American Legion Team. These teams traveled around the County playing other All-Star teams. On Sunday afternoons, we often met at La Palma Park to play our own form of baseball called "over the line."

Social life for Connies and Clems, of course, included hanging out at the Bean Hut and Disneyland. Bobby and his '55 Chevie often seen at the Bean Hut. Car clubs were big in Anaheim in the 50's. There were the Torques, the Roadrunners, the Street Sweepers and more. A group of us formed a short-

167

lived club call "The Disciples". "Hats" and I came up with that name while at a youth meeting at our First Baptist Church. We ended up having a few meetings before the club faded from our lives. We were too busy with sports and other important social activities.

I remember that a group of us from the American Legion baseball team decided to do a little male bonding. We shaved our heads and also drove to the Long Beach Pike to get tattoos. We all had shoulder tattoos. Bobby had the word "Hats" inked into his shoulder. I have often wondered if Bobby kept that tattoo.

I'll never forget Bobby and Dan Turner coming to Jeanie and my wedding in Burbank - in April of 1962. They came to the wedding and then to the church reception hall. I was in the reception line greeting people when Bobby, Dan and I made Momentary eye contact as they waved and passed on by. As I remember that event, I often laugh because I know what they were thinking, "Oh, it's a stuffy church pie and ice cream party." "Let's get out of here". Weddings and receptions in those years were a far cry from what they are today.

It pleases me that Bobby "Hats" Hatfield is being inducted into the Anaheim Alumni Hall of Fame. Great job "Hats". Your Colonist friend, Bill "Swede".

Gary did a great job honoring our father. I really enjoyed reading what Bill had to share in their high school days. I met him at the induction. Very nice guy.

Chapter 54

September 1, 2017

Several years have passed and I have decided to give an update. All is well. I have gotten together with Aunt Jeanne and Kalin over the years and our relationship keeps growing. I have such a busy life between the hubby, kids and grandkids. By the way, I have four now and one on the way in October. Life is great and I still feel as blessed as I did in my previous writings.

One new thing. I decided to go ahead and do the DNA test that Ancestry.com came out with. I had sent it off and had three weeks more to wait. What if there was more family out there that I didn't know about? That would be a wonderful surprise. My husband sent in his DNA too.

There have been so many twists and turns when it came to being adopted and choosing to search. This was a wonderful new avenue.

I received my DNA breakdown about six week later. Wow, I am 51% Swedish, 24% Irish, 10% Italian (no wonder I am a great Italian cook!), 8% English, 2% Europe East which includes Belgium, France, German, Netherlands and finally 2% Spain, Portugal.

I then decided to also do the 23andme.com DNA test. If there were any siblings etc. out there who didn't use the Ancestry website, I could catch up with them there. Those results came back, and they were a little different than the Ancestry test but similar. My closest relative on 23andme is my ½ brother Dustin. No long, lost brothers or sisters have appeared. But I have found a couple of 2nd cousins who are really cool. A shout out to Tammy Greiner and Keith Morgan!!

Wait a minute. Where is the Native American blood that is on my non-identification papers? My birth mother also told me her grandmother was full blood Cherokee. Well, that is incorrect. Hmmm.

Part seven

Final Thoughts

Chapter 55

November 1, 2017

So many things have happened over the last few years. My dad passed away in March of 2015. I miss him like crazy still. He was such a rock and so kindhearted. He always called me, "Shriekly Lynn". He had another heart issue and they had to get him regulated. They were able to fix the problem but in rehab his body was just wore out. He needed to build his strength so he could walk again. It didn't happen. All of the family was gathered by him when he passed on to heaven.

In the meantime, we had moved my mom into assisted living. She couldn't live by herself because we found out she'd forget to take her heart medicine. They kept that a pretty good secret from us.

After my dad died, my mom became pretty obsessed with me. She had taken care of dad for the last 30 years and now felt empty. I'm so glad I moved her just fifteen minutes away from us. I would see her every day after work. She'd be waiting at the front door, sometimes for a couple of hours before I got there. The staff would tell her at 3:30 that I would be there by 5:30, but she'd just wait.

I know that dad's death took a lot out of her both mentally and physically. I always told Dad that I would take care of her and I kept my promise. Mom wanted to come live with us. We had an unfinished basement and she agreed to pay for the renovations to get her moved in.

We were able to move her in August of 2016. Around November, her Alzheimer's really kicked in heavily. I am not going to go into detail, but it was the toughest job I ever had. Hands down!

Speaking of jobs, I was let go at my casino and traded in for a younger version. I can't believe it happened to me. They were letting go of a lot of Managers who had been there for a long time. Over a two-year period, they let 13 Managers go. I was the 12th to be given my walking papers. Luckily, I got severance pay and was able to collect unemployment for the first time in my life.

It turned out to be a blessing in disguise. I had caregivers during the day while I was at work. My son Nick was one of them. He had always been super close to the grandparents. It became too much for him to watch her because she got mean, incontinent and started hitting people. And sadly enough, she was jealous of Nicky's longtime girlfriend. Another sad part of the disease.

Because of my layoff, I was able to spend more time with her. I still kept my wonderful caregivers so I could have a break, but it only got worse, as does the horrific disease. I had a camera on her at night so when she would try to get up, I could run down there. She needed a walker but forgot that she did. In the middle of the night, I would ask her why she was up and she would say she didn't know. I quietly reminded her that she shouldn't get up until she saw the sun shining. That was usually all it would take.

As I keep repeating, it was a terrible disease. She had always been the kindest, loving and most etiquette-ly proper lady I had ever met. And my best friend.

We gave her the best life we could since Dad died. I bought her a Bichon Frise dog name Lilo which brought her a lot of happiness. She adored the little guy and claimed he talked to her. That was okay as long as he made her happy.

One day, my Mom said, "Your brother's birth Dad had a voice like Perry Como." No, Mom. That was my birth Dad.

I made sure my mother ate like a queen, but she kept losing weight. I was told by her Doctors it was because of the Alzheimer's. One day when I was fixing her blanket on her lap and giving Lilo a pet.

I noticed she is staring at me. I said, "What's up Mom?" She said in a low, gritty voice, "I am going to hire a guy to cut you into small pieces with a knife and kill you." That devastated me and I pretended that she didn't say that to me. I told her I was going to fix her a cup of cocoa. I put on The Secret Life of Pets, her favorite movie.

I ran upstairs crying and told my husband that my mother was a b*tch. I might have thrown the F bomb around too. I immediately prayed and ask God for forgiveness. I didn't mean it. I knew it wasn't her speaking to me. It just got to me. I was exhausted and her words came out of nowhere. By the time I came downstairs and served her the cocoa, she completely forgot what she said. She thanked me for her cocoa.

This was a story about my adoption, but I also felt that I needed to include parts of my life. I had a fabulous relationship with my mother and when Alzheimer's took over, it was one of the hardest times of my life.

I lost my Mom June 13th of this year 2017 and I have missed her so much. I am grateful that she was reunited with my Father and fully cognizant after such a long struggle. I don't like being without a mother.

I remembered when her Mom passed away. She said, "It was a pretty weird feeling to now be the Matriarch of the family. I'm pretty sure I don't like it." I have to agree. It's a weird feeling even though her mind was pretty much gone the last month or two. I love you Mom.

I know that my mother has been reunited with my Dad and the terrible disease is no longer a part of her. That was a two-and-a-half-year ride. I wouldn't have traded it for the world though. I was able to get little snippets of her toward the end.

Two nights before my Mom passed away, she was lying in bed with her Bichon Frise by her side. She was very weak but still managed to eat a Fudgsicle, lol. At this point, whatever we could get in her was a good thing. While I was feeding her ice chips, I was talking about shopping. She loved to shop. We always did the Black Friday thing, but it was never called that when I was growing up. Just the day after Thanksgiving Sale. I would go with my Mom and my grandmother. We would fight the crowds at South Coast Plaza.

I chirped on and on for about an hour. We talked about what we were going to give the grandkids for Christmas. The grandkids call me Mimi and my Mom Gigi. She loved that. She just smiled. I told her that we would go to Macy's as soon as she was feeling up to it. She needed a new outfit! We kissed good night as usual and that was really the last good visit we had. She knew she was dying, and I was hoping against hope that we had a little more time.

Chapter 56

It has been a year now, since I have been laid off. I have decided to not return to casino management after an eighteen-year career. There are different reasons for my decision. Second hand smoke for one and I would most likely have to work weekends. After working Saturdays for the last eighteen years, I think I am done with that. I got a taste of how the other side was. I liked it!

Over the course of these last few years, I have also lost a couple of dear friends. Joanne Poole and Jo-Ann and Lloyd Whitaker who were supportive throughout my adoption journey and encouraged me to write this book. I loved them dearly. I had to give them weekly updates which was so cute. They would get so teary eyed when I would tell them the latest. They were big Righteous Brothers fans back in the day. Smart peeps!

Now everything is Facebook, not MySpace. I got on MySpace the other day and couldn't figure it out. It has all changed. It's weird, all of my contacts and emails have disappeared too. That is too bad. It actually says to use Facebook to connect with the people on MySpace.

Bill Medley got a new partner named Bucky Heard in 2016. From everyone who has seen their show, they say the best part is the slide show of Bobby. Of course, people would tell me that, but I have to agree.

I am still close to Kalin and Aunt Jeanne. They are a big part of our lives. Aunt Jeanne and I now text, so that is good. She still does not do computers, so this is a step up, lol! I have to get better at letter writing. Vallyn and Dustin have chosen not to have a relationship with me. I have no qualms with that. To each his own.

I have been able to go to my grandkids (four of them now) sports games and family events. It has been wonderful. I missed so many soccer games over that last few years. I always worked Saturdays. I even got to take a trip to California to pick up a VW bug. My husband and son were going to drive down and I said, "Wait, minute, I can go!" I haven't been able to leave my Mom for the last couple of years.

My girlfriends ask me if I get bored not working. No way! The days just zip by and there is always something to do. It's so nice to have time with my husband. For the last couple of years, I had been caring for Mom and wouldn't see my husband until about 9:30 pm each night. I am enjoying our time now.

I've also devoted a lot more of my time to writing. I knew I had to go through my journey again and add a few more memories. I now have a completed sci-fi thriller and a 12 book children's series that just needs illustrations.

My hopes are to get a book published first so I can write full time. I know finding a literary agent for representation is like finding a needle in the haystack. I will probably go back to work for a couple of years. Since my Mom's passing, Pete and I have done a lot of traveling. We spent a month in Italy which was a once in a lifetime vacation. IT WAS AMAZING. We met some incredible people and learned some great, new Italian recipes which was my favorite to cook. I had started planning the trip while caring for my mother the last few months. It gave me that light at the end of the tunnel and something to look forward to.

Do you want to search? Is it worth all the emotion?

Yes!!!!! I don't regret it for a moment. It is who I am.

Is it who you are?

I have so many people to thank for helping me get through this journey.

To my parents who raised me to be a confident, strong and kind woman, thank you.

To my Search Angels of California, Bob, Donna, Connie and Jan. You have changed my life for the better and it's been a wonderful ride, thank you.

To the musicians who didn't let their fame or ego get in the way of reaching out to me or getting back to me, Reno Bellamy (I love you), Larry Hanson (I love you), Chuck Negron, Peter Noone, Bertie Higgins, Pete Townsend, thank you.

Bill Medley, I thank you for your kindness and acceptance of me from the very beginning. I love you.

To my Hatfield family, thank you for all you have done for me and the kindness you have shared. Aunt Jeanne, I love you and thank you.

To my dear friends who rode this journey with me and supported me, thank you and I love you.

To Oldies Radio Host, Jim Callahan, thank you for all of your support, I love you.

To my husband, Pete. Thank you for all your support over the years. Thank you for initially calling both sides of my birth family because you knew I never would. I love you. You rock.

To my kids, Brandon, Sarah and Nick, I love you. Thank you for all of your support.

To my grand babies - Evan, Olivia, Nathan, Annie and Jordynn, I love you.

August 19, 2020

P.S. I just had a dream that I published my adoption journey. Well, that works for me. It is time.

Now, how do I self-publish? LOL. Amazon, here I come!

On the last few following pages are the side-by-side pictures I found of Bobby and myself, soon after I discovered I was his daughter. I would Google a picture of him while I was at work, then go home and find the picture of his look, in "me" version. I used scotch tape so don't expect anything too professional. XOXO

Bobby
Beaver
His fam
he was
show b
on a lo
the stu
sang i
his firs

"I was
to the
decide
life an
pants
and ev
knees
voice,

Alway
L.A. D
the Or
avid g
tourna
dollars

Bobby
two ch
sons
and a

1940-2003
Excerpts from
Memorial Service

ars

Back
k

1966

The Righteous Brothers
BACK TO BACK

Front Cover

Made in the USA
Middletown, DE
14 March 2024

51494480R00106